RUFFIAN

RUFFIAN
Queen of the Fillies
by Edward Claflin

Scrambling Press

1975
New Canaan, Connecticut

ABOUT THE COVER

The photographs on the covers of this book were taken by William J. Stravitz.

RUFFIAN POSTER

Following the publication of the hardbound edition of this book the publisher received numerous requests for enlargements or posters of the photograph on the front cover. As a result, we've prepared full color posters, 18 inches x 24 inches of this wonderful photograph. To order one, send $4.95 plus 55¢ postage and handling to RUFFIAN POSTER, Box 428, New Canaan, Connecticut 06840.

9   8   7   6   5   4   3   2

For Helen
and her friends

The People Who Helped

There are many, and I wish I could thank them all.

At the heart of Ruffian's story are the people who trained, raced and cared for her. Many are mentioned by name in this book. Whenever possible, I spoke with them personally, and their words revealed something of themselves. I hope I have not abused their trust in any way.

I feel fortunate to have met Mike Bell, Frank Whiteley's assistant, who put aside his doubts about reporters to tell me what he could about Ruffian.

Photographer Bill Stravitz took the pictures which appear on the cover and gave generous, useful advice.

I am most grateful to Ted Lamanno who (as stablehand) answered a barrage of questions and (as instructor) sifted out some of the errors in this story.

Many representatives of the New York Racing Association—Sam Kanchuger, Shirley Day, Frank Tours, Marshall Cassidy and others—took a sincere interest in my research and helped make my task easier.

And some people never stopped helping. Sarah Foote questioned, proofread and listened to headaches. Susan and Peter Tobey gave much of their time and applied their talents to make a story that would be worth the telling.

Edward Claflin
September 1975

RUFFIAN

Born with a Star

Claiborne Farm is located in the heart of Bluegrass country, near the little town of Paris, Kentucky. The farm covers five thousand acres, almost eight square miles, and has some of the finest thoroughbred horses in the world.

During the summer, the landscape looks sunny and peaceful. Rolling meadows covered with blue-green grass stretch in every direction as far as the eye can see. Here and there, a broad-limbed tree casts its welcomed shade over the land. In every pasture horses graze—big stallions, brood mares, yearlings and young foals.

Near the center of this lush farmland is a stately, white mansion with pillars. This house, more than a hundred years old, is the home of the Hancock family, owners of Claiborne Farm for several generations. Raising racehorses has been a family tradition and the walls of the house are lined with portraits of winning thoroughbreds.

At Claiborne Farm there are different stables for breeding, raising and training the horses. In one stable are twenty-six stallions, the father or "stud" horses which service the mares. Another part of the farm holds some three hundred brood mares, the mother horses that give birth to foals each spring. These foals—the male colts and the female fillies—are later separated from their mothers and sent to the Raceland stables as weanlings. When ready to be broken, as yearlings, they go to the Xalapa stables. At Claiborne Farm, raising, breaking and training horses is a year-round activity.

It was on this farm, on April 17, 1972, that a little filly was born to a mare named Shenanigans. This was the filly that would someday be called "Ruffian."

◁ *Mares and foals in the paddock at Claiborne Farm*   Dell Hancock

In the early spring, the busiest man on the farm was James Christopher, the "foaling man." It was his job to keep an eye on the mares while they were giving birth. If necessary, he helped pull the foal out of its mother's body. Then he wiped off its nose so the foal could breathe. He looked after the mare to make sure she would not catch an infection. And if there was an emergency, he called the veterinarian, the horse doctor.

At 9:50 on the night of April 17, Mr. Christopher was with Shenanigans when the mare gave birth.

He looked anxiously at the mare and her foal, but both seemed to be fine. The mare was still breathing heavily. Her flanks were streaked with sweat from the hard work of giving birth, even though it had taken less than half an hour.

She had been carrying the foal for eleven months. She ought to feel relieved, Mr. Christopher thought to himself.

The filly lay beside her mother on the straw. Her skinny legs, awkwardly bent, looked much too long for the little body. She seemed limp and helpless. But Mr. Christopher knew she would slowly gather her strength.

The foaling man carefully began to clean the newborn foal. As he did so, he made some notes to himself. The filly looked all black. When her coat began to dry, however, Mr. Christopher saw that she was actually a dark bay or brown color. There were a few grey hairs mingled in. Slightly above her left hind hoof she had a white ring—a "coronet" that looked like a bracelet around a lady's wrist. And on her forehead was a pointed, white star.

There was one other thing Mr. Christopher noticed about this filly. She was big—bigger than most foals. Maybe he was imagining things, but he thought she looked as big as a colt.

She wanted to get to her feet very soon after being born. She doubled back her long, spindly legs and kicked the straw. But she wasn't panicked or wild. She was calm, as if she knew she could do it.

"Easy, girl," said Mr. Christopher. He didn't try to help her. She would have to stand up on her own, so he simply gave her a little encouragement.

"A little bit more. Okay, up now."

She was on her feet. For a second, her knees seemed to go every-which-way. Then they wobbled into place. She certainly looked awkward but she was standing.

The foal nuzzled up against the side of Shenanigans. The mare swung her head around, as if curious to see who had joined her in the stall. Then Shenanigans, ignoring the foal, began munching hay.

The foal found her mother's teat and started nursing, sucking at the warm milk that would give her strength.

It didn't take Mr. Christopher long to see that the filly was fine. He picked up his bucket and sponge and quietly left the stall, hooking the gate behind him.

As he went out of the stable, Mr. Christopher described her to himself. He would report the birth to Mr. Hancock the next morning. She was darker than her mother . . . big . . . and born with a star.

Mr. Christopher headed across the yard for Barn Number 4. There was a mare he wanted to look in on. After that, he hoped he could get some sleep . . .

Far from Claiborne Farm, in Glyndon, Maryland, two people were pleased and excited to learn that the foal had been born. They were Mr. and Mrs. Stuart Janney, owners of the new filly.

The Janneys owned Shenanigans and they were part-owners of the stud horse, Reviewer. The year before, they had asked Mr. Hancock to breed Reviewer and Shenanigans. They expected to keep the foal for racing.

They knew that a filly would probably not run against colts unless she were outstanding. Fillies were usually smaller and not as fast on the racetrack. Generally the fillies ran in separate races with less prize money offered. As a result, they did not earn as much money as colts.

Nevertheless, the Janneys knew this filly had good parents and they wanted to see her run against other fillies. In order to race her two years from now, there was a lot that had to be done to raise and train their new horse.

The Janneys planned to keep the filly at Claiborne Farm for a year and a half. By then she would be broken and ready for riding. Then they would send her to their trainer, Frank Whiteley. He would get her ready for the racetrack.

A plaque marks the stall where Ruffian was born
Dell Hancock

Now, all they needed was a name. It took them awhile to decide, and the one they finally chose was almost an accident. The name nearly had been given to one of their colts but the colt was sold. So, there was a name left over.

It was "Ruffian."

It meant "a brutal, cruel fellow." Not exactly the name for a pretty lady. With a colt's name, though, maybe she would run like a colt—and win.

The Janneys hoped so.

During the spring months, Ruffian stayed close by her mother. Together they roamed over the meadows. The filly nursed while her mother grazed.

As Ruffian grew bolder, she began running on her own. She explored new places around the paddock and stable. At the least alarm, however, she always returned to her mother's side.

The foal was getting fatter and healthier all the time. She was high-spirited. She nipped at the butterflies that danced over the grass, and she played games with the stablehands when they tried to take her inside.

As the summer days grew hot, the foal was often more content to stand under the shade trees with her mother. As the mare's milk dried up, the filly learned to graze for herself.

Each day was the same. At seven o'clock in the morning, the stablehands came around. They fed the horses and cleaned the stalls. The mares and foals were let out into the field until four o'clock when they were returned to the stalls.

Summer turned to fall. It was September. The mornings were cool and the dew stayed longer on the grass. It was time for Ruffian to leave her mother.

At Claiborne Farm there is one day each year when all the foals are separated from their mothers. That day is called "weaning day."

One morning in early October, the stablehands arrived at six o'clock, one hour before the regular time. At once, the filly sensed that something was wrong. She pricked up her ears. In stalls all around, horses were stamping and whinnying. The filly nudged up against her mother. But Shenanigans had been through this before and seemed unconcerned.

Suddenly there was a shrill whinny, almost like a scream. The filly replied and stamped her little hooves.

A stablehand appeared at the gate. Normally, he would feed her. But this time he didn't. He put a halter and a lead strap around her head and began tugging.

The filly turned her head toward her mother, nuzzling her. The mare turned restlessly in the stall but did not try to help her foal.

"Come on, now, come on," said the stablehand, clucking at Ruffian. He was pulling at her head and she had to turn. She followed the man out of the stable. He closed the gate.

Then she seemed to understand. A loud squeal escaped her. Ruffian tried to turn back. Shenanigans came up to the gate of the stall and stretched out her neck. But she could not reach her foal.

Ruffian couldn't turn back. There were men all around her, speaking in soothing voices, leading her on toward the door. They urged her up a ramp and into the back of a van.

She was packed in with four other fillies. They were smaller than she but their misery was just as great. All were scared, all anxious. Where were their mothers?

The door closed behind them. The floor of the van shook as the truck started up. It jiggled and rocked as they drove away—away from the stall where Ruffian had been born.

When the doors opened, the fillies were in a new and unfamiliar place. They had clean stalls and fresh hay. They had food and water. But their mothers were not there.

"Okay?" shouted one of the hands. "You got 'em in? Let's go get the next load. It's almost six-thirty."

"I'm tired already," replied one of the younger boys.

"Hey, there, get a move on," the driver of the van yelled. The doors slammed closed, the engine started up.

Ruffian turned around in her new stall. It seemed big and empty. And the filly did not like being away from her mother. She gave a loud squeal, though no one came to help her.

At Claiborne Farm, weaning day had only begun.

Foals that have been taken away from their mothers are called weanlings. After a few days, they forget about their mothers and get used to their new lives. They learn to look out for themselves. Throughout the winter, they are given plenty to eat and are let out to run and play.

By the time the spring comes around again, they are one year old. Around the stable, the hands call them "yearlings." They are still too young to ride. But the stablehands talk to them and handle them frequently. The yearlings become used to the human voice and respond to a gentle touch. By the middle of summer, they are ready to begin training.

First, they must learn to carry a rider and respond to the reins and bridle.

One morning in August, two stablehands came to Ruffian's stall. While one man held her and spoke to her, the other stablehand put a strap over her back and buckled it loosely under her belly.

At first, that strap didn't bother the filly. Then they began to tighten it around her girth and ribs. That bothered her.

She turned this way and that, trying to escape from the canvas strap. Soon they had her walking in circles around the stall. All the time, they spoke to her and patted her. Of course, she didn't understand any of it.

Her efforts to shake it off were useless. No matter what she did, the strap stayed on.

That strap was the "surcingle." Every morning the stablehands put it on her so she would get used to the feel of it. Every day they tightened it a little more until the surcingle was as tight as the girth strap on a saddle. Finally, Ruffian seemed to realize she couldn't slip it off.

As soon as she was used to the feel of the strap, the stablehands placed something heavy on her back. It was a saddle without stirrups. It stuck to her like glue. She couldn't shake it off and she couldn't scrape it off either. When she tried to get away from it, the stablehand led her around in circles until she calmed down.

"What're you so excited about?" he asked. "That little saddle ain't no bigger than a cornflake."

But of course Ruffian couldn't understand his words.

Then came the day when a stablehand—really not much bigger than a small boy— was hoisted up on her back. He didn't sit on her like a rider. He quietly lay crosswise over the top of the saddle. Around and around she walked with that limp load on her. She got so used to it, she hardly noticed when he slid on or off.

Each step of training was like learning a lesson in school. They taught her to take the bridle and the metal bit in her mouth. She learned to turn left when there was a pull on the left side of her mouth, and right when the reins pulled her to the right. She got used to the feel of the bridle over her head.

Soon there was a rider on her back, sitting up with his feet in the stirrups and hands on the reins. She was ready for the final stage of her training. She was ready to run.

During her last months at Claiborne Farm, Ruffian moved one last time. Her new home was the training stable called Xalapa.

Now that Ruffian accepted a rider, the exercise boy would take her around the paddock at different speeds. First she walked around the track, just as she had done in the stall. As the boy urged her to go faster, she began to jog or trot. At the quicker pace, she could feel the boy on her back bobbing up and down.

Then she went into a gallop. Her stride became longer and smoother and she seemed to enjoy the speed. Only the bit in her mouth, pulling her in, reminded her that there was a person on her back.

Finally they let her run. Then she seemed to forget everything and everybody. It was almost as if she had been born to run, she did it so easily. She didn't do it for anyone. She ran for herself.

Mr. Hancock, the young master of the farm, stood near the paddock area and watched her. He was surprised at the size and speed of the filly. He noticed how easily she ran, as if she were simply floating along. No one could teach her that kind of grace and speed, not with all the training in the world. It was something she had to learn for herself.

Ruffian was born to be a racehorse. And she was good.

Did she know she was good? Did she understand her destiny?

During her lifetime, many people would ask themselves those questions. She was a horse—not a person. Yet she seemed to possess an intelligence and awareness that went beyond the powers of a horse. She seemed to know herself and her own abilities.

Ruffian was not meant to be an ordinary horse. She wasn't bred or raised or trained for farm work or Sunday carriage-rides. She was meant to run and win. Racing was her business and somehow, people say, she seemed to know that right from the beginning.

The Racing World

Once Ruffian left the peace and quiet of Claiborne Farm, she entered a completely different kind of world. It was the world of thoroughbred racing.

Horse racing is both a risky business and a thrilling sport. The racing world is made up of all kinds of people—owners, trainers, jockeys, racing officials and bettors. It is a world that revolves around horses. It has its own rules, its own language and its own rewards. Someone not familiar with the people and their horses may have trouble understanding what makes that world go around.

The word "thoroughbred," for example. What does it really mean?

People who have been keeping the "family records" of horses for many generations say that every thoroughbred is related to one of three great English racehorses. Those horses were Eclipse, Herod and Matchem. They lived in the 1600s, when the Queen and royal family took an interest in racing. Today there are thousands of thoroughbreds which are descendants of those three stallions.

Careful records have been kept, showing the offspring of each "sire" and "dam," the father and mother horses. When an owner wants to look up the parents of a horse, he can check the "stud book," where each birth is officially recorded.

Besides their family histories, thoroughbreds are set apart in another way. They have thin, strong legs and a graceful shape or "conformation." Most horsemen can tell a thoroughbred from other horses simply by looking at it. Careful breeding has helped make horses with strength and speed.

◁ *Ruffian in the walking ring at Belmont Park. Spectators came early to catch a glimpse of their favorite.*

N.Y.R.A.—Bob Coglianese

Ruffian's parents were thoroughbreds that had been carefully selected for breeding. Her sire, Reviewer, had raced thirteen times and won nine. Shenanigans had raced twenty-two times. The Janneys hoped that Ruffian would inherit some of the best traits of each horse.

The most well-bred racehorse will not be a good runner however, unless it has proper training. Ruffian's trainer would be the most important person in her life.

Trainers instruct all the grooms and stablehands how to take care of the horses. They also select and train the exercise boys who ride the horses during their workouts. When a race is coming up, the trainer and the owner of the horse select the jockey.

Trainers make sure each horse has the proper amount of food, water and exercise all year round. They decide when the horse is ready to race.

Usually an owner relies on the trainer to pick races for his horse. But a trainer also has to be the horse's guardian. He has to know when it is healthy and fit to run. A trainer has to be very alert to know when something is wrong. He should notice right away if the horse is walking with a limp or has a slight fever.

Another important person in a thoroughbred's life is the jockey, the rider of the horse. Jockeys are small and light, so the horses carry as little weight as possible. Most riders are about five feet tall and weigh less than 120 pounds—about the size and weight of a ten-year-old boy.

Jockeys have to be very strong and have a good sense of balance. When a jockey is racing, his feet are in high stirrups close to the shoulders and his knees close to the "withers" of the horse. Perched on those stirrups, the jockey is about five feet above the ground.

During a race, the rider leans forward close to the horse's neck. His head is low, his knees squeezed together, and his seat high above the saddle. When the horse is going full tilt this position is like balancing on your toes on a seesaw.

Jockeys control the horse using the reins. They develop strong shoulders and powerful arm-muscles from this constant strain.

Everything the jockey does is for greater speed. He must diet to keep his weight down. When he races, he keeps his head low so the wind passes over him. He wears thin, light clothing so the horse won't carry extra weight.

Many women as well as men have become jockeys, trainers and stablehands. For a trainer or jockey, these can be well-paying jobs. When a horse comes in first, the jockey and trainer each earn one-tenth of the money won by the horse.

In contrast, grooms and stablehands are poorly paid. They often live in badly furnished rooms near the stables. Sometimes, when a horse wins, the stablehands are given a small part of the money to divide among themselves. For this money, they have to work hard and long hours.

The owners of the horse make the most money but they also take the greatest risk. The prize money, called the "purse," is announced before each race. Every owner wants his horse to win a large purse. If the horse is a winner, the owner can make hundreds of thousands of dollars.

Yet in each race, there is also the chance that a horse may "break down" and be injured or killed. That is the risk the owner takes.

There are other people who take smaller risks—the horse-bettors. At each race thousands of people study the running records of the horses and then place their bets. At the betting window, they get tickets in exchange for their money. If they win, they turn in their tickets and get double, triple or more of their money back.

If they lose, they may come up with wild ideas to explain why their horses failed. Horse-bettors are noted for their crazy excuses.

But whatever the outcome, betting always adds to the excitement of the race. And the crowd always has some favorites, the horses that people like to see run and win.

At the center of all this excitement are the horses. Over a distance of a mile or more, the thoroughbred is the fastest land-animal in the world. A well-trained thoroughbred can run nearly forty miles per hour. Most of the horses weigh about one thousand pounds—half a ton. To make that much weight move so fast requires tremendous power.

The legs of the runner take a terrible beating. When a horse runs its fastest, each hoof touches the ground at a different time. For an instant, that leg carries the entire weight of the animal and rider. It is rare for a thoroughbred to break a leg. Frequently, however, as a result of the tremendous strain of running, they have minor injuries and so their legs need constant care.

Some thoroughbreds run in "steeplechase" races over obstacles like fences and bushes. Others run "turf" races on grass. The most popular and fastest races are on dirt tracks.

The tracks are oval-shaped, with long "stretches" and rounded "turns." They have a hard, firm base and a softer, sandy surface. When the track is dry and firm, it is a "fast" track. If it gets wet and muddy, the horsemen call it a "sloppy" track.

Usually there are five to a dozen horses entered in each race. They are lined up in a starting gate, a steel structure that can be rolled into position on the track. The gate has a number of narrow stalls. At the "post-time" the horses are lined up in these stalls, ready to run. When the starter gives the signal, all the stall-gates open, and they're off.

Races vary in distance from about half a mile to a mile and a half. The distance a horse runs may depend on its ability and experience. Some horses are sprinters that run well for short distances but tire after three-quarters of a mile. Others can keep up a good pace for almost any distance and are considered the best runners.

On a racetrack the distance is measured in "furlongs." Each furlong equals one-eighth of a mile. A three-quarter-mile race, for example, is six furlongs. There are poles around the track to mark these distances and clockers check the speed of the horses as they go by the poles.

A young, starting horse begins with short races, then builds up to longer distances. The most famous races, like the Kentucky Derby, are always more than a mile.

Today, horses start running as two-year-olds, when they are still considered very young. Many horsemen believe that a two-year-old is not mature enough to start racing. They say the horses are not fully developed, and there are many chances of an accident. Most trainers race two-year-olds to give them early exposure. Then, by the time they are three, they are in the peak of form.

Some horses race in later years and a few still win at the ages of seven or eight. But most thoroughbreds retire from track racing after their third or fourth year. After that, most successful race horses are sent to a breeding farm.

Male and female horses usually do not run in the same races. Generally colts are stronger and faster than fillies. The races they run are faster and more popular so they are likely to earn more money during their lifetimes. There are separate races for fillies, where they stand a fairer chance of winning. Once in awhile, a filly comes along that can beat the colts. In the history of horse racing, this has happened only a few times.

In the United States, hundreds of horseraces are held throughout the year. Of course, some races are much more important than others, and every owner wants a horse that will win the big events. For colts and fillies, the most famous races are the Kentucky Derby, the Preakness and the Belmont Stakes. These three make up the Triple Crown and few horses have been able to win all three races in one year.

There is also a New York Triple Crown for fillies. The races are the Acorn, the Mother Goose and the Coaching Club American Oaks.

Rarest of all are the match races. For a match race, two owners must decide to run their horses. No other entries are allowed. Usually these two horses are the best in the country and so are singled out for this special kind of test.

Since 1900, fewer than a dozen match races have been held in the United States.

Although people come to the racetrack to win bets, they also come to admire horses. They watch the beautiful colts and fillies parading around in the paddocks. They point out the qualities of the horses and criticize their bad points.

There is always excitement and tension around the racetrack. People are thrilled to see the power and determination of the horses as they run for the finish line. Even the quietest spectators begin shouting when their horses come down the final stretch. Each person in the grandstand wants his "favorite" to win.

But there are also *horses* who want to win. They show it. People recognize it. These are the horses which have been considered great.

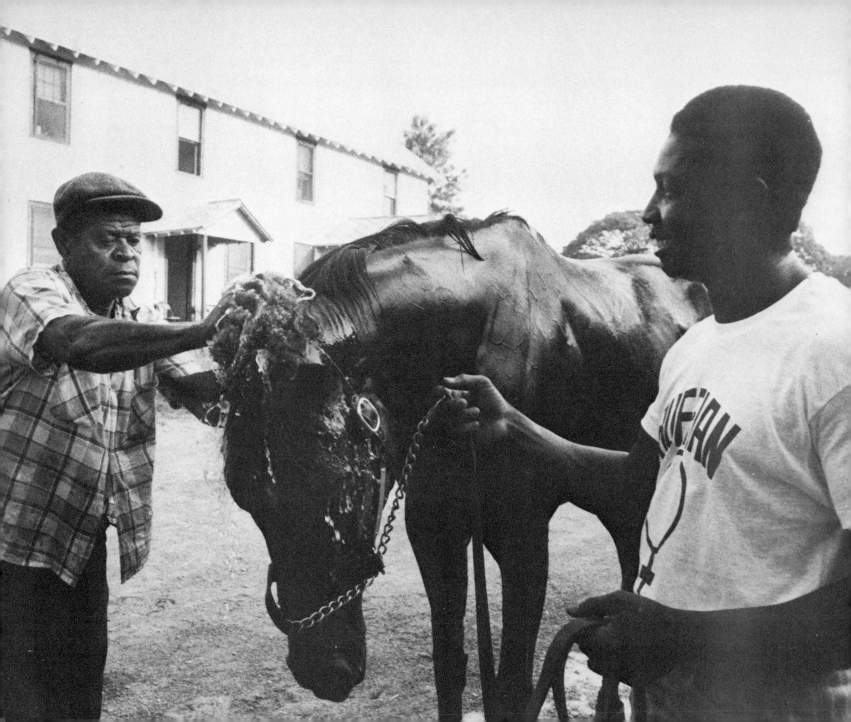

The Spirit of Her!

On November 15, 1973, Ruffian was sent from Claiborne Farm to a training stable in Camden, South Carolina. Her trainer would be Frank Whiteley. If all went well, she would be ready to race by the following spring.

It was a long ride. All day the van swayed from side-to-side as it sped along the highways from Kentucky to South Carolina. When the door opened, Ruffian was in a new place. Instead of the rolling meadows of Claiborne Farm, she saw dusty fields and dark pine forest. Strange faces surrounded her. Unfamiliar hands tugged at her halter. Cautious, a little frightened, she walked down the ramp.

One of the first people she saw was Dan Williams. Dan would be Ruffian's groom.

Born and raised in South Carolina, Dan Williams was a stocky black man. He was fifty-seven years old when Ruffian came to the stables.

Dan had a kind face, but a lot of sadness showed up in it too. When he was a young man, his wife had died and left him with four children. With the help of his friends and relatives, he'd managed to take care of the kids and send them through college. Then, not long ago, one of his sons was killed in Vietnam.

Dan spent most of his waking hours looking after the horses. He didn't make any fuss about the work. In fact, it seemed as if he didn't pay attention to anything that wasn't his business. But appearances could be deceiving.

◊ *"Washing down" Dan Williams gives Ruffian a good splash behind the ears while rider Squeaky Truesdale holds up her head.*   N.Y.R.A.—Joseph DeMaria

*Alert, ready to race, Ruffian poses in front of the clubhouse.
The silver plate on her bridle carries the names of her sire and
dam — Reviewer and Shenanigans.*   N.Y.R.A.—Bob Coglianese

In fact, Dan noticed a lot of things. He'd spent most of his life working with horses, but he knew a lot about people too. He knew which people he liked and didn't like, yet he was careful to treat them all the same. He knew which horses had spirit and which ones didn't, but when he took care of them, he followed Mr. Whiteley's instructions, showing no favoritism. He usually kept his ideas to himself.

Dan had been working for Mr. Whiteley for six years when Ruffian came along. The trainer knew that Dan was good with the horses. "He knows his way round a horse's head" was the way Mr. Whiteley put it. And that was why he asked Dan to take care of Ruffian.

Long afterward, Dan recalled that November day when he first saw the filly.

"She impressed me right away," Dan said. "She was just a different horse. She was *all* horse. Looked like nothin' you ever saw. The spirit of her!"

From the beginning, Dan seemed to have a special kind of understanding with the new filly. She played games. She'd go after him in the stall, try to nip his arm or grab the seat of his pants.

"Look out, there," Dan would warn. They glared at each other. Ruffian would pull back and look at him like she knew she'd done something wrong.

Then Dan would turn around, and the next thing you knew, she'd nip him again.

Dan knew he couldn't hit her. No one could. She would fight right back. But he had another kind of warning, with the flat of his hand along the side of her neck. That told Ruffian he was there. She would turn around as if she were going to eat him. Then he grabbed her under the chin and pulled at the place where she liked to be scratched. He could groom her by himself and Ruffian wouldn't kick at him. He could even tack her—put the bridle on over her big, proud head—and she wouldn't object.

Sometimes the other stablehands came around her too. After a few incidents,

On a racing day, Dan leads Ruffian to the Belmont track. Many spectators came early to watch the filly go through her paces.

N.Y.R.A.—Bob Coglianese

though, they realized Ruffian was going to be Dan's horse. If someone else tried to come into the stall, she would kick out. The way she nipped might be playful, but if she went for your arm—that hurt.

Sure, she might be playing. But how could you tell the difference?

Unless you were Dan. He seemed to know. He would bully her, and she would try to get her revenge. Still, Dan Williams knew his way around a horse and he found a way to get on her good side.

Arising before dawn everyday, Dan was in the stables by five o'clock. First he checked the feed tub to make sure she'd cleaned it out. The night hand had fed her at four o'clock.

Then Dan unhooked the water bucket and trudged out of the stall. He dumped whatever water was left outside the stable. Then he swished out the pail, filled it at the tap and carried it in to her.

"Look out," he'd say, coming under the stall gate. "Gettin' so big, there ain't room for no one else," he grumbled as he hoisted the heavy bucket up to the hook.

Dan went and got a pitchfork and started lifting the dirty straw out of the stall. He tossed clumps of straw and manure onto a square of old burlap. Then he folded up the burlap, loaded it on a wheelbarrow, took it to a pit and dumped out the dirty straw.

Just about the time Dan got the stalls clean, Mr. Whiteley had him take Ruffian out for exercise. All that fall he walked her for hours around the paddock, wearing off the fat of a yearling.

Dan also had to wash and brush her and check her legs. If her legs became hot with fever, Mr. Whiteley would tell Dan to wash them down with cold water. Or Dan would stand her in ice water till her legs cooled off. If she'd nicked herself in the stall or paddock, Dan would brush her with iodine. Sometimes he applied cooling plasters of mud wrapped up in paper towels to keep her legs comfortable.

Promptly at eleven o'clock the horses started whinnying up and down the line. They knew it was feeding time. The stablehands had already measured out the special mixture of oats and bran. For each horse there were two or three quarts. They would eat more in the afternoon.

Everyday, Dan turned over the feed a couple times to bring the moist grain to the top. Then he slung the feed tub around where Ruffian could reach it. The filly began eating greedily.

In the middle of the day, Dan had some time off. Later he returned to the stable to walk and graze the horses and clean their stalls. At four o'clock he fed Ruffian her third meal of the day.

Dan was used to the work and the schedule. Yet, as he got older, it wore him down more. Those water buckets were heavy and sometimes his arms ached at the end of the day. He went about his chores at a steady pace, often feeling tired.

Having been with horses so much, Dan knew that each one was different from any other. He couldn't help liking them as he got to know their ways. They showed their spirits in different ways, showed character in different ways. As the years went on, Dan watched them pass through the farm. Somehow he always felt attached to each of them.

He liked that young filly, Ruffian. More than that, he admired her. One of the hands said, "She's a queen." To Dan that sounded about right.

"Dan, bring her on out here!"

It was Mr. Whiteley calling.

"Yes, sir," Dan replied. He already had the bridle on her.

"Hey, now, stay in line," Dan said gruffly, as he led Ruffian out of her stall.

It was February and Ruffian was a two-year-old. In a few more months she would be on the racetrack.

It seemed to Dan as if they had spent the whole winter walking her. Sometimes Dan, sometimes Mr. Whiteley, sometimes both in the same day, just walking her around for hours.

Then came the "ponying." Mr. Whiteley got on the stable pony, took Ruffian by the halter and lead strap and let her gallop easily while he rode beside her around the track.

Now, at last, it was time to see her run.

Dan led Ruffian away from the white barns and out to the half-mile track. He could hear Mr. Whiteley talking to the exercise boy.

"Once easy," Mr. Whiteley was saying. "I know she's fast. Don't want her run out. Keep her under wraps."

Mr. Whiteley held a stopwatch in his hand. He gave a leg to the exercise boy, who mounted easily onto Ruffian's broad back. The rider slipped his toes into the high stirrups. He gave a tug to the reins—so slight you couldn't even see his fingers move.

Ruffian responded. Daintily, almost casually, she turned in a circle. Then the filly and rider started off.

Ruffian didn't seem nervous at all. She accepted the man on her back. She seemed to enjoy feeling the dirt track under her hooves.

This ride wasn't a race. It was more like a question. How fast could this filly run?

Mr. Whiteley nodded and the exercise boy took Ruffian around once at a gallop. As they passed by a second time, Mr. Whiteley nodded again and the boy rose up from the saddle, legs squeezed together. The filly began her run.

Standing nearby, Dan saw Mr. Whiteley press the starter on the timing watch. Then he looked at Ruffian.

She was already so far away it was almost impossible to tell her speed. If he hadn't known better, Dan would have thought she was barely trying. She looked graceful and she ran smoothly. She gave the strange impression of just floating over the ground, without working or straining.

As she came around, Dan watched her dark body flashing against the line of trees behind her. Suddenly he realized how fast she was moving. She was going like wildfire.

Together Dan and Mr. Whiteley watched her go around the track. In seconds, her graceful body was surging past them. The rider was pulling her in. The trial was over.

Mr. Whiteley looked down at his stopwatch. He didn't tell Dan how fast she was and Ruffian's groom didn't ask. But there was a tight-lipped smile on Mr. Whiteley's face.

"Some filly," said Mr. Whiteley.

"Yes, sir," said Dan. "She's all horse."

Mounted on the stable pony, Frank Whiteley glances at his stopwatch as Ruffian runs for home.
N.Y.R.A.—Joseph DeMaria

High on a Horse

Frank Whiteley didn't need a stopwatch to tell him that Ruffian was a special kind of horse. He knew that just by looking at her.

Frank Yewell Whiteley, Jr. was well-known in the racing world, both for his abrupt manner and for his skill in raising horses.

It was his manner that people noticed first. A short man, with red complexion and white hair, Frank Whiteley came into a conversation like a prize fighter. All his sentences were short jabs, many were commands. He could be harsh. He didn't like boys with long hair and he certainly wouldn't hire one. He didn't like people disturbing his horses. He wouldn't tolerate sloppy work.

When Mr. Whiteley walked around the stables, he walked fast. He looked like he'd mow down anyone who got in his way. He wore a light-colored, starched shirt and creased pants, his clothes never seeming to get wrinkled or dirty no matter how much he worked.

When he came in, around five o'clock in the morning, he was puffing on a cigarette. A stiff, straw hat was pushed down low on his forehead. Generally, he'd toss the cigarette aside before he came into the stable.

"Okay, bring her out," he'd say. To an outsider, his orders would have sounded like a secret code. But the stablehands knew what he wanted. They did as he said.

Frank Whiteley believed that the horses always came first. He'd learned that lesson a long time ago when he first began training horses.

◁ *Yates Kennedy "breezing" Ruffian during a morning workout. Kennedy rode Ruffian in South Carolina when she began training for the 1975 racing season.* N.Y.R.A.–Joseph DeMaria

William J. Stravitz

Frank Whiteley

Frank had grown up in Centerville, Maryland, where his father was sheriff of Queen Anne's County. At eighteen, he started training his own horses for the little half-mile races. Those races were called the "frying pan and leaky roof circuit." Trainers had to do their own cooking right by the stalls. And they had to patch the leaky barn roofs when it rained.

In such a situation, the trainer sometimes had to make sacrifices for his horses. Sometimes young Frank had to pass up a meal so his horses could be fed. That's where he learned the rule: "Horses come first."

By the time Ruffian came along, Mr. Whiteley was close to sixty years old. Now he took care of thoroughbreds for a number of owners. And he'd trained some winners. His son, David, had joined him in the business, then started training on his own. Mr. Whiteley had one home in Camden, South Carolina. During the summer, he and his wife Louise rented an apartment near the Belmont Park racetrack in New York. But wherever he lived, Frank spent most of his time with thoroughbreds.

Frank Whiteley was with the horses as much as the grooms and stablehands were. Usually, he was the first one at the stable in the morning and the last to go home at night.

He noticed everything. If a horse had a slight limp or even just a piece of straw in its tail, Frank noticed it. The horses couldn't talk, but their trainer knew when something was bothering them.

Lots of times, he knew, people could bother horses. Mr. Whiteley didn't encourage reporters or strangers to come around the stalls where they might get the horses upset. At the racetrack, he exercised them early in the morning when there wouldn't be a lot of spectators. He was usually the last trainer to bring his horse out of the stable before a race. He figured there wasn't much point in getting a horse upset before it ran.

People around Mr. Whiteley got used to his tough manner. The stablehands respected him and even liked him. He had character.

But he also had secrets. It seemed everyone who met Mr. Whiteley wanted to know those secrets. He was famous for keeping them to himself.

The truth was, Mr. Whiteley didn't have any secret formulas that made him successful. He just kept a couple things in mind. First of all, a horse wasn't meant to be kept in a box all day. One morning workout wasn't enough. They needed some variety every day.

Second, horses were a lot smarter than most people gave them credit for. If a horse had heart, you had to bring out the best in him. If a horse had class, you had to respect him.

Heart and class—those were two things every trainer looked for in a horse. Those qualities weren't easy to describe in words, not unless you had a feeling for horses.

Mr. Whiteley knew that some horses were considerably smarter than others. Some had more courage. You'd get horses that were lazy, others that were high-strung, and some that were reckless. When you'd been with the horses long enough, you usually could figure out why they acted one way or another.

Still, it wasn't easy to figure out why some horses had class and others didn't. It was a quality you'd sometimes find in human beings who knew they were good or knew they could win. How could a horse know it?

Some horses did. You could tell by the way they carried themselves and the way they acted. Horses like that would put everything they had into winning. And they did it for themselves, not for a carrot or a lump of sugar.

Mr. Whiteley knew that Ruffian was a horse like that. She had class.

"I don't get high on a horse," Mr. Whiteley often said. He meant that he didn't pay more attention to one horse than another. And he didn't get overconfident.

Training horses is a long, slow process of building them up, getting them to the point where they're ready to race. Each one needs individual attention, and each one is on a different schedule.

Mr. Whiteley assigned people to the horses and told them what to do.

Sometimes the exercise boys would take the horses out jogging, going at a slow trot around the ring. When Mr. Whiteley thought the horses were ready, they would gallop. Sometimes they had riders and other times the exercise boy rode alongside on a pony holding the horse's lead strap and halter.

Finally came breezing. When a horse was breezing, the rider mounted like a jockey and ran the horse near top speed. But they couldn't be run like that every day.

Mr. Whiteley always watched the horses closely during the workouts and sometimes he "ponied" them himself. If a horse got tired and didn't eat well, Mr. Whiteley tried to find out what was wrong. He eased the schedule, went back a step. On the other hand, if a horse was getting fat and lazy, it was time to work him a little harder.

There were always problems to watch out for. Horses could get bad habits like running too close to the rail or breathing through the mouth instead of the nostrils. They

Frank Whiteley, wearing his favorite straw hat and riding a stable pony, leads Ruffian out of the sheds. Her rider, John ("Squeaky") Truesdale, helped train Ruffian as a two- and three-year-old.

N.Y.R.A.—Joseph DeMaria

could get stomach aches from twisted intestines. Or fevers, swollen ankles, or bucked shins. These were all things that a trainer had to watch for.

All during the spring of 1974, Mr. Whiteley kept his eye on Ruffian. She was doing fine. Her legs were in good condition and she was right on schedule. If she had a fault, it was that she wanted to run too fast. The exercise boys had to hold her in or she'd just run away from them.

But you couldn't really call that a fault.

In spite of himself, Mr. Whiteley was beginning to get high on that horse.

By May of that year, Mr. Whiteley had moved most of his horses up to the Belmont Park racetrack just outside New York City. They were ready for the racing season.

For Ruffian there were new sights and sounds. The track was different and she saw more people around.

But otherwise her life was unchanged. Dan Williams came to her stall the same time each morning. She had her morning workout and purple clover to munch at the end of the day.

Meanwhile, Frank Whiteley was considering her future. At the end of the day, when the stable was quiet, Mr. Whiteley sat outside the tack room in a canvas-backed, folding director's chair. He opened the condition book, folded back the cover and began studying.

The condition book was compiled by the racing secretary of the New York Racing Association. It set forth the "conditions" for each race, stating which horses were qualified to run. It was up to the trainers and owners to decide where they wanted to run their horses.

The Racing Association scheduled a number of races that would be for fillies alone. Some of them were restricted to two-year-olds like Ruffian. Others could be run by older horses as well. The sweepstakes or "stakes" races had the largest purses, but a horse had to qualify for those.

Stakes races for fillies included the Fashion, Astoria, Sorority and Spinaway. If Ruffian won those races, she could earn over one hundred thousand dollars her first year. If she were fast enough, she might even go on to race colts at the end of the season.

But that was a long way off. Mr. Whiteley didn't believe in looking beyond the next race. For Ruffian the "next" race was the first race.

It should be a short distance. She should run against other fillies who were as young as she was. The race would give her some experience, a chance to run against other horses. It was an important race and Mr. Whiteley took his time making a decision.

Finally he found what he was looking for.

A race for fillies was scheduled for May 22. It was a short distance, five and a half furlongs or less than three-quarters of a mile.

Mr. Whiteley got up from his canvas-backed chair and looked into Ruffian's stall. She was munching her clover. May 22—her Maiden Race. How would she like it?

He was pretty sure she'd like it fine.

Now to find her a jockey.

The Maiden Race

On May 22 Belmont Park was bustling with activity. All morning long, trucks and limousines and Cadillacs went in and out of the stable area as the owners came to check up on their horses. The Pinkerton men, security guards at the track, kept careful watch at the gates and stables. These horses were valuable and it was their job to protect them.

The sports reporters arrived on the scene and talked to the trainers, trying to get the inside story on one horse or another. Out in the paddock area, groundsmen were raking up. Under the shade trees, venders put the Coke on ice and waited for the hot dogs to arrive. On the main track the trucks circled all morning, raking the sandy surface and sprinkling water to keep the dust down.

In the jockeys' locker room everyone seemed to be calm. Jack O'Hara, the ruddy-faced clerk of scales, checked off the jockeys' names as they came in and said a few words to each of them.

"Vasquez," he said to one. "Who's this 'Ruffian' you're gonna ride? One of Frank Whiteley's horses, I understand."

The man he spoke to, Jacinto Vasquez, was about half the size of Jack O'Hara. Vasquez was South American, from Panama. He had light brown skin, jet-black hair and flashing eyes. Jack O'Hara knew from experience that the jockey's temper could be as quick as his eyes. Now and then they'd had a little run-in.

◊ *After a winter of care and training, a confident Ruffian walks to the track*

N.Y.R.A.—Bob Coglianese

This morning, Vasquez was smiling.

"She's a good filly. You watch," he said.

Then Vasquez went into the locker room.

He's a good jock, Mr. O'Hara thought to himself. If only he could keep his temper under control. It seemed like he was always getting suspended for rough riding or breaking some kind of rule. Each suspension meant seven days without work. Even Mr. O'Hara had to fine him once when the jockey swore at him.

Perhaps that fighting spirit helped him win races.

In fact, Jacinto Vasquez would never have been a jockey if he hadn't gotten in trouble in the first place.

It all started when he was thirteen. He was born on a farm in Panama, one of ten brothers and sisters, but he soon left for the city. One day, he got in a street fight. He was arrested. Just when he was about to be clapped into jail, a woman stepped forward. She said she worked in the open-air market nearby. If the police would let Jacinto go free, she would see he didn't get in trouble again.

That woman was the mother of Heliodorus Gustines, a jockey. One Sunday, she took Jacinto to the racetrack. Though he had never seen racehorses before, he knew right away that he wanted to be a jockey.

Mrs. Gustines found him a job in the stables. At first he just groomed horses and "mucked out" the stalls. Three months later, he began riding the horses during workouts, then racing them. After winning a number of races in Panama, he was brought to the United States as an apprentice.

The street fighter was still in him. During his first year of racing in the U.S., he was suspended 140 days. Often it was for "rough riding," trying to force other horses aside during a race.

Sometimes, when he was suspended, Jacinto said he didn't know what he did wrong. He said he was innocent. But the truth was, he didn't like losing. He just didn't like to get beaten by another rider. He fought back.

In time, he learned to control that fiery temper and put his energy into hard racing. It paid off. By 1974, the time of Ruffian's Maiden Race, he was one of the top ten jockeys in the country. He was just thirty years old.

Jacinto Vasquez, Ruffian's jockey, rode her in all but two races. Vasquez is five feet three inches tall and weighs less than 120 pounds. N.Y.R.A.

Vasquez had ridden other horses for Mr. Whiteley. He had a lot of respect for the trainer. This year, Vasquez had his eye on Ruffian from the moment she came up from South Carolina. Vasquez would show up at her morning workouts. He wanted to get up on her and try her speed. Mr. Whiteley would tease him.

"You can run her in the afternoon," he'd say. "But not now. I don't want to use too much of her up."

Finally, Vasquez got his chance. Before the Maiden Race, he took her for a workout. He broke her out of the gate, ran for a quarter mile, and then began to pull her up. She just wanted to go faster and faster. It took all his strength to slow her down.

"I never run a horse like that," said Vasquez, recalling that day. "She was a horse that knew what she was doing. She was all horse when she run the first time."

In the jockeys' room, the riders put away their decks of cards and began to get ready for the afternoon races. They stepped on the scales to check their weights. A few went into the sweat room to lose a couple more pounds.

Vasquez lay down on the table to get a rubdown before the race. He wasn't nervous. None of the jockeys seemed nervous. They joked with each other and shared friendly insults.

But underneath this, there was a little tension. Some of the men would be riding two or three mounts that afternoon. Once they got on the track, they would be competing with each other, competing for fame and money. And there were dangers. They were riding thousand-pound animals at speeds up to forty miles per hour. One mistake, one bad fall could be disastrous.

But Vasquez didn't think about that. He put such thoughts aside. Once he got on the horse, only the race was important.

It was getting close to post time. Vasquez began dressing for the race. He slipped on the thin breeches, the brightly colored silk shirt. He pulled on the polished leather boots and combed back his hair. When he left the room, he was carrying his riding helmet and a leather whip.

But he knew he wouldn't need the whip. Not for Ruffian.

In the stable area Dan Williams and Mr. Whiteley were putting the bridle on .

Ruffian. Mr. Whiteley waited as long as possible before he brought her out of the stable. He knew there would be people all around the track and he didn't want her getting excited too soon.

As it turned out, he didn't need to worry. Ruffian was so calm she almost seemed lazy. Mr. Whiteley knew this was a good sign. Let her save her energy for the race.

"You do good out there," said Dan. "Just move along like he tell you."

Ruffian nipped at Dan's sleeve. Her groom didn't want to play, however. He took her by the bridle. She ducked her head.

As Dan led Ruffian out to the paddock, she kept her head low. Her right eye was a little bloodshot, giving her a wild look.

Vasquez met them in the paddock.

He had wondered how she would be during this first race. Even when they ran perfectly during a workout, you couldn't be sure what they'd do during a race. From the moment he looked at her, Vasquez knew it was all right. He liked her coolness. She was saving her fight for the track—and so was he.

Vasquez mounted her.

"Try and make her relax," said Mr. Whiteley. Vasquez nodded. He knew Mr. Whiteley was talking about the first part of the race, when she started running.

Vasquez didn't walk her around the paddock. He rode Ruffian straight out to the track.

The crowd was disappointed. The spectators wanted to have a look at the filly. But most of them had put their bets on the other runners—Suzest, or Garden Quad, or Alpin Less. And they thought "Ruffian" was an odd name for a filly. Sounded like a colt's name.

Vasquez had an easy time of it. Ruffian was calm all the way to the starting gate and she didn't balk as she went into the stall. She was in the Number 9 position, near the outside.

The other fillies stirred nervously as they found their places. They were all young and inexperienced, yet Ruffian acted as if she'd been racing for years.

Vasquez was ready to go. He crouched forward on her neck, his feet in the stirrups, hands tight on the reins. He might have to hold her back in the beginning.

Once she opened up, there was no telling what she could do.

The starter gave a signal and the gate opened.

Looking back on it, Vasquez realized that Ruffian ran that first race the same way she ran every other race in her life. The only difference was that she had a little trouble at the gate—she "broke" a little slow. After the start, though, she surged ahead. She went around those other horses like they were standing still. Once she was in front, she pulled farther and farther ahead.

That was the way she would run her whole life. She never seemed to feel any pressure. She never let up, either. She grew more confident, more in control. She didn't worry about the other horses and there was no reason why she should. All she had to do was run a little faster and the others would be left behind. It seemed as if she could always run faster.

The most amazing thing about her was the way she changed. During the race she was a different horse. It was as if she threw off one personality and took on another as soon as she went in the starting gate. She always seemed calm, almost bored, before the race. The moment the gate opened, she exploded into action. It was a complete transformation.

In her Maiden Race, Ruffian finished fifteen lengths ahead of all the other horses. Vasquez never touched her with the whip. After the start, he didn't do anything except let her run.

Her speed was a miracle. Running five and a half furlongs, she tied the record speed for the Belmont track. One reporter called it "the greatest race ever run by a first-time starter." To top it off, that "starter" was a filly.

Jacinto Vasquez was smiling steadily as he rode Ruffian back to the stands. This Maiden Race wouldn't make him famous. It wouldn't earn him a lot of money. That didn't matter. He just wanted to ride Ruffian again.

◁ *True to form, Ruffian finished 4¾ lengths ahead of Sir Ivor's Sorrow.*

N.Y.R.A.—Bob Coglianese

1 *May 31, 1975, the Mother Goose race at Aqueduct. Ruffian (second from left) started in the Number 6 position.*

2 *Leaving the gate, Dan's Commander (Number 7) stumbled and pitched forward, tossing her rider. That left Ruffian on the outside . . .*

3 *. . . moving up on the inside horses. She kept the lead over Point in Time (Number 5) . . .*

4 *. . . caught up with Sun and Snow . . .*

5 *. . . passed Gallant Trial, Sweet Old Girl, Sir Ivor's Sorrow . . .*

6 *. . . and swept into the lead. Vasquez crouched low as she raced for the finish line.*   William J. Stravitz

He soon had his chance. During the spring and summer of 1974, Ruffian raced four more times. Vasquez was her rider twice more that season.

She won every race. She set new track records for each of the stakes races. No filly before her had ever run so fast in those events. No filly had ever won so easily.

After her Maiden Race, she ran in the Fashion Stakes. She won by six and three-quarter lengths. The next three races were won by nine, two and a quarter, and thirteen lengths.

She never fell behind during any race. She never waited until the end before pulling ahead. In each race she took the lead and stayed there.

By August, she had won more than $134,000. People were calling her "Superfilly." They'd never seen anything like her. Horses like that came along once in a lifetime.

Then people began to talk about her future.

End of a Season

By August people were already beginning to whisper about a "match" race between a colt and the brilliant young filly. The best colt and best filly in a single race—it was an unheard-of idea. Ruffian, however, was an unheard-of kind of horse. Clearly, she could not run with the fillies much longer. No filly could touch her.

Which colt should she run against?

One choice seemed obvious. That colt's name was Foolish Pleasure. He was a two-year-old. By August he'd won five races and lost none. In that respect their records were exactly the same.

But there the similarity ended. According to the track times, Ruffian was faster than Foolish Pleasure. Running three-quarters of a mile, she finished more than a whole second faster than the colt. What would happen when they ran together?

That was something people wanted to see. The idea of a match race began to catch on. Ruffian and Foolish Pleasure—they seemed to be made for each other.

But one person didn't think so. That was Frank Whiteley.

Ruffian was only two years old. She hadn't run any distance greater than six furlongs, just three-quarters of a mile. She needed some age on her and she needed more experience.

Mr. Whiteley was bringing her along, doing it his own way. When people started talking about a match race, he turned a deaf ear. Let them talk all they wanted—it wouldn't change his plans.

Still, Mr. Whiteley had to admit he was beginning to get high on this horse. He was starting to look beyond the next race. He knew that was a mistake. He shouldn't count

With flying hooves Ruffian rounds a turn and heads for the homestretch. Vasquez used the whip on Ruffian only once during her entire racing career.

N.Y.R.A.—Bob Coglianese

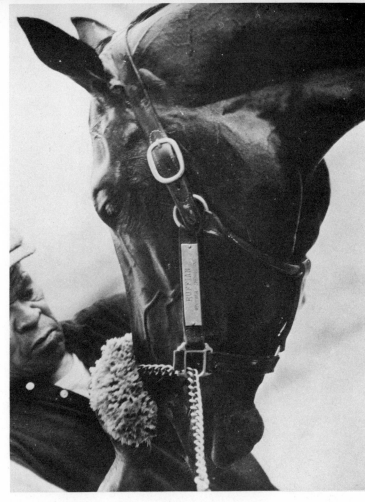

After a morning run, Ruffian gets her muzzle washed by groom Dan Williams.

N.Y. Daily News Photo

on too much. Anything could happen. But he'd never had a filly like this one. She was so fast, she almost scared him sometimes.

Mr. Whiteley's friends said he got nervous when he had a good horse, and right then he was nervous. Next spring was the Kentucky Derby. Maybe he was beginning to think the unthinkable. A filly in the Derby? Impossible. There hadn't been a female runner in fifteen years. And no filly had *won* that race in the past sixty years.

Mr. Whiteley set his mind on the race coming up. Ruffian was entered to run in the Frizette Stakes on September 26. The purse was $100,000. It was the biggest race of her career.

September 26 came and went. Ruffian did not run.

On the morning of that race, Mr. Whiteley got to the barn at five o'clock as usual. He checked the other horses, then peered into Ruffian's stall.

There was something odd. She had been fed a couple quarts of grain at four o'clock that morning. Though normally her tub would be cleaned out, it was still full.

Mr. Whiteley looked at her carefully. Her head was drooping. There was sweat on her flanks.

The trainer took her temperature.

The thermometer read 101⅗.

Later that morning Mr. Whiteley put in a call to Kenny Noe, the racing secretary. "She's got a fever," said Mr. Whiteley. "You'll have to scratch her."

On his schedule Kenny Noe put a dark line through Ruffian's name. He knew the fans weren't going to go for this. He asked Mr. Whiteley what he'd done for her.

"Gave her some of my country medicine and some aspirin," the trainer replied.

The racing secretary didn't know whether to believe Mr. Whiteley or not. But he knew it was a cruel blow for the trainer. And Mr. Whiteley told him he didn't think Ruffian would run in the next race, either.

Mr. Whiteley made a second call that morning, this time to the Janneys, Ruffian's owners. They had come to the city for the race and were staying near the track. The news was a bitter disappointment to them. Ruffian probably would have won easily if she'd run the race. If she missed other races that fall, she would lose out on the chance of being "Horse of the Year." They knew, and Mr. Whiteley knew, that Horse of the Year was an award this filly deserved.

On September 26, twenty-five thousand people turned out at Belmont Park. They almost groaned aloud when they heard that Ruffian had been scratched.

By noon, Ruffian seemed to be feeling better. Her fever went down. Still no one, not even Mr. Whiteley, knew when she would run again.

The Frizette was won by a horse named Molly Ballantine.

By Friday morning, the day after the race, Ruffian's fever was down to normal, between 99 and 100.5 degrees. She was also eating better and cleaned her feed tub. Still, her troubles were far from over.

When Mr. Whiteley went into her stall, he noticed that Ruffian stumbled slightly as she turned around. It was hardly noticeable but Mr. Whiteley was sure he'd seen it.

The trainer took her out of the stall at once and walked her around. She did not take another mis-step. Puzzled, he returned her to the stall. He decided he wouldn't run her until he found out what was the matter.

A day or so later she took another bad step as she was in the walking ring. Mr. Whiteley had seen enough. Taking her back to the stable, he called the track veterinarian, Dr. Prendergast.

"I want her x-rayed," said Mr. Whiteley, though he couldn't say exactly where the problem was. "I know it's her hind section somewhere," said the trainer.

Dr. Prendergast began that day. Before he was done, he had more than one hundred x-rays of her hindquarters and back legs.

He studied the pictures carefully. All the bones seemed to be in good shape. Could it be that Mr. Whiteley was wrong? A few bad steps could mean anything. Maybe it was something minor.

But the trainer was stubborn. His sharp eye and his instinct for horses told him this might be serious. He wouldn't run Ruffian until he knew what the trouble was. It was up to the vet to find out.

Dr. Prendergast returned to the pictures again. He went over them one by one. Finally, the careful examination paid off.

In the lower, right pastern—a bone just above the hoof—he detected a hairline crack.

Dr. Prendergast went to the stable at once. He knew he would find Frank Whiteley there.

The trainer took the x-ray picture and held it up to the light.

"That's it," he said shortly. "What do we do about it?"

"She'll have to be in a cast. Probably for six weeks or so."

Mr. Whiteley nodded. At least they'd found out what was wrong. But it wasn't reassuring news. It definitely meant the end of Ruffian's racing season. And it might mean the end of her career.

When a horse fractures a leg, it is much more difficult to cure than a broken leg in a human being. There are many reasons for this.

Each of the bones and joints carries a great deal of weight. The movement of the legs during running puts a lot of stress on the complex joints. When any kind of fracture occurs, it can have an effect on the entire system of the horse.

Sometimes there is shock caused by loss of blood or sudden injury. During shock, the body races to make up for the loss of blood—and often loses the race. Severe shock can cause death.

Even if there is no shock at all, a horse cannot be treated like a human being. When a person breaks a leg, the cure is usually simple. The patient goes to bed. The doctor puts a cast on. Then the patient walks with crutches while the leg is still in the cast. When the bone is healed, the doctor takes the cast off and the patient starts to use the leg again.

Unlike a person, a horse does not understand what has gone wrong. When the doctor tries to help, the animal may fight back.

Also, horses cannot remain lying down for long periods of time. When they do their blood does not circulate properly and waste matter builds up in their bodies. Their nerves do not get enough blood, they stop working and the horse loses control of its muscles. Sometimes paralysis sets in.

Finally, a horse weighs much more than a human patient. The leg that is broken has to support one-quarter the weight of the horse. Unless there is a very strong cast on that leg, it will break again under that kind of load.

In the past, nearly every horse with a broken leg was "put down" or killed at once. There didn't seem to be any way of saving an animal that could neither stand nor lie down.

New ways have been found recently to save these horses. Veterinarians use slings, drugs and hydraulic tables that tilt from side-to-side. The injured horse can be given a sleeping drug. The doctor can operate on the leg and put a cast on it before the horse wakes up.

However, there are still dangers. After the operation the horse has to accept the cast. If he begins kicking, the cast will slip and the break will open up again. The horse must stand up again soon after the operation so he won't be paralyzed. The horse has to stand *quietly,* as well.

Some racehorses have recovered completely after long operations. A few have lived to race again. Yet even today many horses have to be put down after breaking a leg.

With only a hairline fracture, Ruffian did not need surgery. She did need to stand quietly.

Dr. Prendergast put a "jelly" cast on her right hind leg. The cast, only a little stiffer than an elastic bandage, could be changed frequently.

The doctor wondered whether she would accept her confinement. If she kicked the stall, the fracture could become worse.

The bone that was cracked, the "pastern," was just above her hoof. Fortunately, she had not injured any of the joints in that leg.

Above the pastern there is a very delicate joint where the pastern is attached to a larger bone. At this joint there is a pair of bones called the "sesamoids." When a horse runs very fast, the sesamoids can slip out of place. Sometimes they are chipped or shattered by the shock of the other bones.

When Dr. Prendergast checked the x-rays, he looked carefully at the sesamoids. He knew that fractures often occurred there.

Not this time, though. The sesamoids looked fine. The fracture was only in the pastern.

After Dr. Prendergast put the cast on her leg, Ruffian responded well. She didn't try to kick out or resist. The doctor thought it was surprising that a horse like that would stand still. She was a model patient.

With luck, the leg would heal in a couple of months.

The Winter of Doubt

Some people thought Ruffian would never return to her old form. They knew she had a minor injury. However, they pointed out that it happened at a crucial time in the life of the filly.

Between the ages of two and three, a horse is still growing and changing in many ways. Every horseman knows that a young colt or filly can be altered completely by a winter on the farm. Sometimes a horse that is totally unknown as a two-year-old comes back for an outstanding season as a three-year-old. But the reverse is also true. A filly with a lot of promise can lose it during the winter rest. Even if Ruffian came back, track people said, she might be a completely different horse.

And that was a big "if." As the fall months dragged on and the round of season races drew to a close, the word got out that Ruffian was still in a cast. People shook their heads.

Foolish Pleasure, meanwhile, won two more races in September and October. While Ruffian was hardly beginning to walk again, Foolish Pleasure was already running mile-races. It was hard to imagine that there had been the possibility of a match race. Those dreams were over, people thought. Ruffian would have to go a long way just to recover lost ground.

If people around the racetrack were having doubts, that didn't influence the hands around Frank Whiteley's stable. They knew Ruffian would come back. She was doing

◁ *Ready for a workout, Ruffian steps along briskly as Yates Kennedy gives her a few words of encouragement.* N.Y.R.A.—Joseph DeMaria

fine. As soon as the bone healed, they would move her down to South Carolina. With a winter rest in Camden, they thought, she'd come back as strong as ever.

And if Mr. Whiteley had any worries, he kept them to himself. He sent a copy of the x-rays to Dr. Alexander Harthill, an expert horse doctor in Lexington, Kentucky. Dr. Harthill confirmed that the fracture wasn't too serious. Nevertheless, he wanted to see more x-rays before Ruffian ran again.

Dan Williams and Mr. Whiteley kept close watch over Ruffian. They couldn't fault her as a patient. When the cast was changed, as it was every other day, she didn't start nipping or bucking. She turned her big eye on Dan and stood still until the "doc" and the trainer had done everything they wanted to.

You just had to admire her, Dan thought to himself. Up to the time she hurt herself, she'd been working out every day and racing at least once a month. She'd been at the peak of form—a young, athletic horse that wanted to run.

Now she'd simply turned it off. All she was doing was standing still, hour after hour, in a stall scarcely big enough to turn around in. Her entire training had been aimed toward getting her out of that box. Now she had to remain in it. It was amazing she took it so well.

Around the stable, the other hands gave her almost as much attention as Dan.

"She's a perfect lady," they used to say. They watched out for her.

Ruffian never let the others into her confidence the way she did with Dan and Mr. Whiteley. But that didn't matter. Merely being around her the stablehands felt like they were being honored. They were in her court and that meant something.

Ruffian's feed was reduced to four quarts a day. Without daily exercise, she couldn't eat more or she'd get fat.

That amount was about one-third her usual meal, consequently she was always hungry. She would munch a lot of hay. One of the stablehands, a girl named Mary Jane, fed Ruffian some candy now and then.

Even Frank Whiteley had to admit that he spoiled Ruffian a little. He let her eat more hay than she should have.

When Dan Williams came to Ruffian's stall, he didn't play games any more, nor did he boss her around. He talked to her in that low, grumbling voice of his. She stayed still.

Jacinto Vasquez stopped by to check up on her progress and talk to Mr. Whiteley.

"I wanna ride that filly next year," said Jacinto.

"She'll be ready," said Mr. Whiteley. "Just keep out of trouble."

Vasquez made a sour face. No more suspensions, he promised himself. No more fighting, no more rough riding. He was gonna be good. He didn't want any other riders on her but himself.

The mending took about as long as the doctor had predicted. In late November the cast came off for the last time. It had been on almost eight weeks.

Now they could move Ruffian to Camden.

As far as Dan Williams was concerned, it was time to go. Life near a big city didn't seem like much to him. Up north, he was closer to his grown-up children—the daughter in New Jersey and the son in Hartford. But he'd be back.

Down south it would still be warm. The farm would be pleasant this time of year.

If all went well, if Ruffian started running like she was supposed to, Dan knew he would see plenty of racetracks next season. He suspected he'd also see plenty of trophies.

Almost as soon as they got to Camden, Dan and the other stablehands had to set up the "Porta-paddock." This was a portable fence about nine feet high that broke down into sections. They could set it up around any area, depending on how much room they wanted to give the horse.

Inside the fence, Ruffian could move around without anyone leading her. It allowed her a workout without running too fast or too far.

At least, that's what it was meant to do.

But Ruffian was starting to feel frisky. As soon as she got in the Porta-paddock, she wanted to show off and play. She started digging. By the end of the morning, she'd made a nice hole right in the middle of the paddock area.

"Okay, fill it up," Mr. Whiteley said to the stablehands.

They went in with shovels and filled it up.

The next day, Ruffian dug her hole again.

Jogging around the track, Ruffian notices some bystanders and turns her head. Her rider is Squeaky Truesdale.

Squeaky rises high in the stirrups as Ruffian breaks into a gallop.

That went on day after day, until it got to be a joke around the stable. The hands grew good and tired of filling in her hole every day, yet there wasn't a blamed thing they could do about it. She was just playing.

There was another game she played that sometimes scared everyone. That game was called running.

Starting from a standstill, Ruffian would suddenly leap forward and tear around the paddock. That game was fine when she was on the racetrack. In the small area of the Porta-paddock, though, she looked like she was going a good bit too fast.

She'd head for the fence. When it looked like she was about to crash head-on, she would stop, turn, and leap away, barely inches from disaster.

Neither Dan nor anybody else could talk her out of that playful habit. She knew her own abilities better than anyone. She knew how fast she could stop and turn, and she had perfect balance. She was as agile as a ballet dancer.

The only thing she didn't know about was that almost-invisible crack that was supposed to be healing. There was no way to tell the patient that she still needed rest.

With Ruffian running full-speed, the 165-pound rider had to use all his strength to keep the filly in check.

N.Y.R.A.—Joseph DeMaria

By January the bone seemed to be thoroughly mended. Mr. Whiteley sent some x-rays to Dr. Harthill. The veterinarian reported that the pastern was as good as new. The doc also had praise for the patient. "She went through a period of stress as if she understood we were trying to help," he said.

With this favorable report, Mr. Whiteley decided to resume training. He asked Yates Kennedy to be her exercise boy. The so-called "boy" was actually a fifty-nine-year-old man who weighed 125 pounds. During the summer, he drove a horse-van in the north. He rode horses during the winter. When he got a call from Mr. Whiteley, Yates hurried south to begin training Ruffian.

A curious reporter from the *Daily Racing Form* was on hand when Ruffian took to the track again. He asked Yates Kennedy what it was like to ride her.

"She's got strength, poise, confidence," replied the rider. "There's no way to describe the feeling. It's like she has a way of saying, 'I am the greatest.'"

Mr. Kennedy went on to tell the reporter he didn't care if he never drove a van again.

Though Mr. Whiteley's most important concern was Ruffian's recovery, the new year brought an award for the filly and her trainer.

Ruffian, it was announced, had won the Eclipse Award for young fillies. Next to "Horse of the Year" it was the highest honor she could receive.

The Award dinner was on January 31, 1975, Frank Whiteley's sixtieth birthday.

"Ruffian has been both a pleasure and a heartbreak," Mr. Whiteley told a reporter. "Perhaps for the first time in my life, I was looking beyond the next race."

That was a lot more than he usually told reporters. At the Award dinner, Mr. Whiteley didn't talk about the future. He didn't want to hear anybody's ideas about match races or colt races or big stakes. Yet those subjects were hard to avoid.

Everyone was aware that the Eclipse prize for colts also was being awarded that evening. That award went to Foolish Pleasure.

Word had got around, as well, that Ruffian was in training again. It was too late for her to run in the Derby and she might not be ready for colts until the summer. Then it would be time for her to meet Foolish Pleasure.

Needless to say, Mr. Whiteley didn't have much patience with that kind of talk.

February passed quickly. By March Ruffian was running as well as ever. It was apparent that the winter's rest had done her good.

In the middle of March, Mr. Whiteley took four of his horses up to Saratoga. Then he turned around and went right back to get Ruffian. Her first race was scheduled for April 14 at the Aqueduct racetrack. Jacinto Vasquez would be her rider.

Ruffian won four races at Aqueduct that spring. In the first race, she led the closest horse by five lengths. Her time was as fast as ever.

The news got around. Ruffian was back. The queen of the fillies had returned! She was going for the New York Triple Crown.

Calm and poised, Ruffian heads for the starting gate for the Acorn Stakes — the first step toward 🖒
winning the New York Triple Crown for fillies.

N.Y.R.A.—Bob Coglianese

Mr. and Mrs. Janney (left) accept the Stakes award cup after the Acorn race on May 10. Jockey Jacinto Vasquez (center) and trainer Frank Whiteley (right) joined Ruffian's owners in the winner's circle.   N.Y.R.A.—Bob Coglianese

On April 30, she won the Comeley Stakes by eight lengths, setting a new stakes record for that event. On May 10, she raced in the Acorn Stakes, broke another record, and won by an even bigger margin. She won the "Mother Goose" on May 31, leading by thirteen lengths and setting yet another record. Each time, Jacinto Vasquez was her jockey.

Ruffian needed one more race to win the Triple Crown from the fillies. On June 21, she returned to Belmont Park racetrack for the Coaching Club American Oaks race.

Thirty-one thousand people turned out to see her. It was a sunny afternoon at Belmont. Ruffian was sporting a new pair of $35.00 shoes, size five racing plates, perfect for the fast New York racetrack.

When the gate opened, she took the lead. She stayed there. A horse named Equal

Change came up on her flank. Vasquez didn't move a muscle. Ruffian simply strolled away. She got about three lengths ahead and flew over the finish line.

The Triple Crown was hers, easily. There was nothing more for her to win among the fillies. It was time for the queen of the fillies to face the colts.

After the victory, owner Stuart Janney leads Ruffian to the winner's circle at Aqueduct racetrack.

N.Y.R.A.—Bob Coglianese

A Match With Fate

Ruffian's record was astounding. In all of her ten races, no filly had ever been ahead of her for more than a few seconds. Ruffian had equaled two speed records at the Belmont Park racetrack. She had set seven new stakes records. In her tenth race she had tied the all-time record for the Coaching Club race. Ruffian had won ten races by a total margin of eighty-three lengths.

How should she meet the colts?

In the clubhouse of the New York Racing Association there were long hours of discussion. Jack Dreyfus, the president of the Association, and Kenny Noe, the racing secretary, made numerous phonecalls, wrote letters and talked over plans. They spoke to Mr. Greer, the owner of Foolish Pleasure. They discussed the possibilities with the Janneys and Mr. Whiteley.

Reporters hung around the clubhouse, anxious for the first news. Finally they were rewarded. Word leaked out. A day later it was official.

The great filly, Ruffian, would meet the winner of the Kentucky Derby, Foolish Pleasure, in a match race on July 6 at Belmont Park.

In the racing world, the news of the Match Race was greeted with smiles of satisfaction. So it had come at last!

Unlike most races, where a number of horses are qualified to run, the match is arranged between the owners and trainers of only two competing horses. In times past,

◁ *Ruffian finished the Mother Goose in record time, leading the nearest horse (Sweet Old Girl) by fourteen lengths. The purse was $100,000.*
N.Y.R.A.—Bob Coglianese

this was the most popular kind of racing. One owner would say to another, "My horse is better than yours." Then the two owners would place their bets and run the horses against each other.

Today such races are rare. Match races are arranged only when there are two horses which are clearly outstanding. It is not a betting race, since the odds are not very great on either side. It is a race to find out which horse is faster.

For this reason, a match is the toughest kind of horse racing there is. The horses must have great speed and stamina, with the determination to win. In ordinary races, a horse can stay behind during the race, then surge ahead at the end. Or the jockey can use tactics to gain a position that gives him an advantage. Those kinds of tactics don't pay off during a match race, though. The only way to win is to run faster and harder than the other horse—all the way.

For the match between Ruffian and Foolish Pleasure, the purse was unusually large. The winner of the Match Race would get $225,000, nearly one-quarter of a million dollars. The horse that came in second would earn $125,000. However, the racing officials agreed that they would not have to pay the second horse if it did not finish the race.

The announcement of the Match Race was followed by a storm of publicity. Newsmen, bettors and racetrack officials, everyone who ever followed horse racing, had their minds on the great event. Even people who had never heard of Ruffian or Foolish Pleasure were fascinated by the race. Reading every detail of Ruffian's history, they looked forward to the race as some kind of celebration. It was the race of the century, with Ruffian as the favorite.

In all the excitement before the Match Race, one fact was uppermost in everyone's thoughts. This wasn't a race between two colts, nor a race between two fillies. It was a "boy" vs. "girl" match, a race between a colt and a filly. That had a special significance.

Many people thought of Ruffian as if she really were a "girl." The fact that she

Foolish Pleasure, mounted by John Nazareth, working out before the Match Race. As the day of the big Match approached, racetrack officials reported the colt's time after each morning workout.

N.Y.R.A.—Joseph DeMaria

would be pitted against a powerful male horse, and the possibility that she might win, suggested a special kind of victory. It would be like a young, beautiful girl suddenly appearing in the Olympics and running faster than any man on the track. People imagined that beautiful girl racing across the finish line with her hair flying, as graceful as a ballerina and as strong as a warrior. They imagined her smiling, bowing and accepting her trophy. Best of all, they imagined that the time on the clock would be the fastest in the world. If she ran true to form, the "girl" could set a record that no "boy" could beat.

There were a lot of jokes about it. There were men who laughed and said it was impossible. No woman had ever won against men in the Olympics, they pointed out. No filly could beat a colt like Foolish Pleasure.

Wives, girlfriends and daughters argued against them. They were certain the filly would win. Just give her the chance. When the Boy *vs.* Girl Match was over, they said, the men would have to admit the girl was better.

So the arguments raged on, with neither side using many facts or figures to back up their claims.

To those who knew horses and racing, however, the match had nothing to do with "boys" and "girls." It wasn't a contest between human runners. It was a race between a good colt and an extraordinary filly. And they looked at the records.

In the first place, Ruffian was bigger than Foolish Pleasure—about three inches taller and sixty pounds heavier. The differences in height and weight were not great but in a close race these differences could give her a slight advantage.

According to her racing history, Ruffian was also faster than Foolish Pleasure. People who compared their running times found that Ruffian covered three-quarters of a mile in about 1:09—one minute and nine seconds. On the same track, Foolish Pleasure had finished the same distance in nearly 1:11—one minute, eleven seconds. On paper, that meant that Ruffian would be a couple seconds ahead of Foolish Pleasure when she finished three-quarters of a mile.

When Ruffian began her career, there were some people who doubted she could run long distances at high speed. Now she had a record that proved her endurance. Running a mile and an eighth, she was a whole second faster than Foolish Pleasure. It looked as if Ruffian was a faster runner for a race of any length.

But that was only on paper. In other respects, Foolish Pleasure had a slight advantage. He had run fourteen races. Ruffian had only ten on her record. He had more experience than Ruffian and had met with stiffer competition. He knew what it was like to run all-out with a horse following close behind.

In the days before the Match Race, all these numbers and facts and guesses were discussed by the people around the track.

In New York and nearby states, thousands of people began making plans for the big day at Belmont Park. Television stations got ready to broadcast a program that might have a bigger audience than the space flight. At Belmont Park racetrack, the growing excitement could be felt in the air as the great Match Race approached.

On the morning of July 6, the sky was grey with clouds. The Match was to be the eighth race and people prayed that the rain would hold off. Ruffian had never run on a muddy track before. If the track got soaked through and sloppy, there was no telling what might happen to her.

Although the Match Race would not take place until six o'clock, people began pouring into the grandstands early that morning, long before the first race. They wanted to hear the news. When was Ruffian's last workout? How fast had she run? Were both horses in good shape?

Soon the announcement came. Ruffian and Foolish Pleasure had been checked by the track doctor. Pulse, temperature and heartbeat were normal for both horses. There were no signs of lameness. The two thoroughbreds were in perfect condition.

Spectators breathed a collective sigh of relief. The Match Race was still on. That's what they had come for. Now they could sit back and enjoy the other races. And hope that it didn't rain.

All morning and early afternoon, they continued to arrive. A steady stream of bettors moved back and forth from the windows. In the early races, some won and some lost, yet to the losers it didn't seem to make much difference that day. There was only one race they were really interested in and the odds favored "the girl." Even if she won, they wouldn't turn in their tickets. They would keep those tickets as souvenirs of the greatest race of a lifetime.

Braulio Baeza, Foolish Pleasure's jockey for the Match Race. John L. Greer, owner of Foolish Pleasure, asked Baeza to ride the colt after Vasquez decided to go with Ruffian.

N.Y.R.A.

After the fourth race, a sprinkle of rain fell on the stands. People held their breath. Then it stopped.

The track was still dry and fast.

In the jockeys' locker room, Jacinto Vasquez was getting dressed.

There are no heroes in the jockey room. For two of the riders, though, this was a day unlike any other. They did not dare think too much about the race coming up. They refused to be nervous. Jacinto Vasquez and Braulio Baeza both knew that only one of them could win that day. In the eighth race Vasquez would ride Ruffian and Baeza would ride Foolish Pleasure.

As far as Vasquez was concerned, the Match Race already had forced him to make one big decision. The jockey had been Ruffian's rider from the very beginning of her career. He had missed only two of her races in 1974—both times because he was under suspension. Vasquez knew he was "her jockey" and he felt a sense of loyalty.

The trouble was, Vasquez was also the jockey for Foolish Pleasure. He had ridden the colt to victory in the Kentucky Derby and in ten other races.

When the Match Race was planned, Vasquez had to choose between Ruffian and Foolish Pleasure.

He chose Ruffian.

In Stable 34, that day began like any other. Around five o'clock, Dan Williams came into Ruffian's stall.

"Hey, now," he said, and there was the usual battle of wits as he tried to get by her without being nipped. Her feed tub was cleaned out. A good sign.

Ruffian wanted to play but Dan wasn't interested.

"Take care o' yourself," he said. "You got to run good like you do."

A short time later, Dan led her out of the stall into the yard. Frank Whiteley took up a hose, turned the spigot, and trained a stream of cold water on Ruffian's legs. She lifted a hoof, set it down again and bowed her head.

One of the stablehands leaned on his rake and looked over at her. She was perfect. The doctors said so, the fans thought so. She knew it herself. Just look at the way she stood there.

For a fleeting moment, the stablehand and Dan Williams and Frank Whiteley were all thinking the same thing. She was going to win. They'd never say it aloud. That would bring bad luck. And they knew that luck played a part in the race. On that grey morning, they also knew there was no horse in the world like Ruffian. They thought she was magnificent.

"Okay," Frank Whiteley said, turning off the water.

"Let's go," said Dan, pulling gently on her lead strap.

The stablehand started raking again.

Most of the day went by like that. A few strangers passed by outside Ruffian's stall, talked to Frank Whiteley or peered in at the gate. Dr. Hartley, a track doctor, payed a routine visit and examined Ruffian.

At eleven o'clock the horses up and down the line started whinnying and Ruffian poked her head out. Feeding time.

In her last workout before the Match Race, Ruffian starts out from Stable 34 at Belmont. Squeaky wears a "Ruffian" t-shirt with a circle-and-cross insignia for the female horse.

N.Y. Daily News Photo

In the stable area, it was a restful afternoon. Now and then a security car cruised slowly past Stable 34. Across the way, in the dingy grooms' quarters, some stablehands with the day off began a card game. Later, they looked at their watches and headed for the track.

Two pigeons passed by the stable window. Ruffian perked up, swung around to look at them. They were gone already. She returned to munching her hay.

Not till the day was almost over was there any change in the routine. Mr. Whiteley came in again and placed some elastic bandages over Ruffian's hind legs. Since last fall, she'd worn them in every race. They helped protect and support her hind ankles so she wouldn't hurt her leg again.

Dan Williams followed Mr. Whiteley. They began putting the bridle on her. She fidgeted in the stall.

She'd guessed it. This was a racing day.

By the time she came out of the stable, she was ready to go. And the people around her asked those questions they'd wondered about since her birth. How did she know she was a racehorse? What was it that set this filly apart?

Even to the people who understood her best, those things remained a mystery.

Mr. Whiteley led her out of the stable and up the hill to the walking ring. He was joined by Vasquez. The jockey spoke to Ruffian, then talked to Mr. Whiteley.

"Take her to the lead," said the trainer. "Let him try and catch you."

The trainer helped Vasquez up on Ruffian. She stood in the stall on one side of the walking paddock. Vasquez walked her once around the ring, then out through the center passage of the grandstands toward the track. There were people everywhere, talking excitedly. The excitement didn't touch her. She felt a tug on her reins and walked onto the track.

Mounted on Ruffian, Jacinto Vasquez headed across the track toward the starting gate. His mind was on the race. He had walked the track the day before and he knew the course by heart. He also knew the danger-spots.

The race would begin in the "chute," a short, straight leg that entered the oval track at the backstretch. About halfway down the chute, there was a slight ridge where another track crossed over. This was deep near the rail and a horse could lose footing. Vasquez knew he'd have to stay away from the edge of the track at that point.

The second danger-spot lay where the chute entered the main track. On the backstretch, the surface was a little more firm than in the chute. Ruffian would feel the change. She'd have to get used to the different surface before he could let her go. But after that . . .

Vasquez smiled to himself as Ruffian approached the starting gate. She'll have to fight for this one, thought Vasquez. He was glad to be fighting on the same side.

The big, steel framework of the gate loomed in front of them. It had space enough for a dozen horses, at least. But today, only two horses took their places.

Ruffian was on the inside, nearest the rail. One empty stall separated her from Foolish Pleasure. They waited but a moment.

When he left Ruffian, Frank Whiteley joined his wife, Louise, in the clubhouse. He was recognized by many people—owners, trainers, and "regulars" at the track. They nodded in his direction and wished him luck.

He wore his straw hat as usual and there was a tight smile on his lips. He wasn't looking ahead to winning. He didn't have to. The race was right here, right now, and if there was anything to prove, Ruffian would do it herself. Everything he could have done for her had already been done. After the race, he'd go on doing the same. But right now, it was all up to her—as he knew it had always been. All Mr. Whiteley had to do was watch the race. He squinted his eyes, prepared to do just that.

Dan Williams didn't feel comfortable with all the people around him, but he'd been through enough races that he'd found out the best place to stand. He was down near the rail, right by the finish line, where he could see Ruffian when she came around. He knew she'd be first and knowing that gave him a good feeling. As far as most people knew, Ruffian was still a secret. Dan knew her and so did Mr. Whiteley but he suspected they were the only ones. If she ran this race right, everyone would know what she was. That was all right. She might be everyone's favorite then but she'd still be *his* horse. She'd go to the winner's circle and get the trophy, and everyone would cheer. Then she'd come back to the stable and belong to Dan.

"She's at the gate," someone said behind him.

"Ladies and gentlemen," said the announcer. "It is now post time."

The gate opened.

The start. Coming out of the gate, Ruffian turned slightly toward the rail, and Foolish Pleasure (Number 2) nosed ahead of the filly. A moment later, Ruffian leapt into the lead.   N.Y.R.A.

As Ruffian broke from the gate, Vasquez felt her turn sharply toward the inside, almost heading for the rail.

She recovered instantly, but the other horse had a slight edge. Ruffian leapt forward and in an instant the two horses were even. Then the filly passed Foolish Pleasure.

Vasquez rode high on her neck, elbows in, head up, balanced above the saddle. Ruffian worked under him, pounding the earth as she surged ahead of the other horse. It was a mad, frantic dash down the sandy track. Vasquez felt the tension in every part of his body.

But his head was cool. A slow start, he thought to himself. The first danger-spot was coming up. That ridge across the track. They had to stay near the middle to avoid it.

As they headed toward that ridge, Vasquez saw Baeza moving in with Foolish Pleasure. The other rider wanted Ruffian to move closer to the rail, where the track was soft. The fighter in Vasquez said, "No!" and Ruffian said, "No!" She didn't budge an inch, even when Foolish Pleasure was close enough to touch them.

Then both horses were out of the chute, heading down the backstretch. The second danger-spot was past, thought Vasquez. Ruffian hadn't changed her pace at all. Now there was just the straight track in front of them and Vasquez let her go.

The pace was tremendous. The jockeys were riding thunder. It seemed as if all that energy would explode.

Then Vasquez felt the wonderful transformation that took place when Ruffian found her stride. Without any loss of speed or determination, she changed the wild pace, shifting to great leaps that hurtled her forward. Now she was as smooth and graceful as a bird in flight, her powerful muscles eating up the ground with each stride. She was smooth, she was easy and she was winning.

As they passed the quarter-mile pole, Vasquez began to pull her in a little, thinking Baeza would do the same. They had a mile to go yet. The pace was miraculous. But it couldn't go on like this for another mile.

Evidently, Baeza thought it could. Foolish Pleasure crept up next to Ruffian, their strides locked together like marching soldiers.

Ruffian swung along, her gait unchanged. Vasquez knew she would not allow Foolish Pleasure to pass by. The track was her property. She allowed no one in front of her.

Just beyond the pole that marked three-eighths of a mile, Ruffian started to surge ahead. Under him, Vasquez felt that power turning to energy, the energy to motion, the motion to new speed . . .

Vasquez heard a sound like a twig snapping. Ruffian changed her stride. For an instant, it seemed like she would topple over.

Vasquez thought quickly. That sound, the change of pace meant one thing—a break. If the break was high up, she would fall. She could not carry herself on three legs. If they went down together, they would be trampled by Foolish Pleasure. They were trapped between the rail and the killing beat of the colt's hooves.

Vasquez fought to keep her up. He struggled to stay on. That was all he could do.

Somehow she kept running. That wasn't what Vasquez wanted now. He pulled her back, trying to control her with the reins. She did her best to respond.

A moment before, horse and rider had concentrated on winning. Now Vasquez told her the opposite—"Slow down! Slow down!"—while he prayed for the other horse to pass them.

In seconds, she had slowed. But it seemed ages before Foolish Pleasure passed by and rushed onward. Baeza glanced sideways, remaining low on his horse's neck, pressing on Foolish Pleasure toward the finish. He had heard the snapping sound. He knew Ruffian was out of the race. Yet a jockey had to finish.

As Ruffian took her last few steps, her head bobbed up and down as if she were drowning. What no one could see at that moment was the terrible damage she inflicted on herself. Hours later, the doctors would try to reconstruct what happened during those agonizing seconds.

Ruffian had broken both sesamoid bones of her right leg. First the bones had been wrenched out of place. Then they were shattered by the ramrod force of the other bones. The effect was like hitting a piece of glass with a sledgehammer.

The fragments of broken bone were as sharp as broken glass, too. As Ruffian ran forward, the pieces of bone sliced through her flesh. Without support behind the crucial

leg joint, her tendons gave way and the hoof turned up like a ski. During the last moments of the race, Ruffian's right front hoof was completely useless. Incredibly, she ran directly on the long bone of her leg. It was as if a person, having broken a foot, kept running on the ankle.

With each step the cuts got deeper in her leg and the wound filled with grit and sand from the track. While she struggled to stay up she had to shift her weight to the left front leg. The added weight on that one leg caused her ankle to buckle. Bent, that ankle struck the ground and was cut open. She ran seventy yards in this condition. With each step the damage grew worse.

Only moments had passed since Vasquez heard the leg snap. Once Foolish Pleasure was gone, Vasquez guided Ruffian across the track. He leapt from her back with the reins in his hands.

She reared back, tossing her head. Blinded with pain, she fought the small man who held her by the reins, pitting her weight against his.

She lost the struggle. The man was sound and she was crippled. Her front legs were covered with blood.

Vasquez held on, tears streaming from his eyes.

The instant Ruffian began to slow down, Dan Williams ducked under the rail and started across the track. Under his feet, the sand felt deep and slow. Before Ruffian stopped running, Dan had reached the inside rail. He sprinted across the infield.

Frank Whiteley started down from the stands. His shoulders were hunched forward, his hat pulled down low on his forehead.

From his box seat high above the track, Mr. Janney kept his eyes fixed on Ruffian.

Foolish Pleasure rounded the final turn and started down the homestretch. He was no longer running hard. There was no reason. The colt galloped across the finish line alone.

◊ *Ruffian broke down before reaching the half-mile post on the backstretch. In the grandstands, dismayed fans watched Foolish Pleasure pull away while the crippled filly limped to a halt.*
Wide World Photos

On the far side of the track, the track ambulance drove out through a break in the hedge. Dr. Manuel Gilman rushed across the infield and approached Ruffian. He saw at once she was in dangerous condition. She was standing on three legs and bleeding badly. Dirt covered the wounds. The right hoof, smeared with blood, was loose and unusable, like something no longer a part of her. The misery was terrible to see.

The first task was to get her standing on four legs again.

Then they'd find out whether they could save her.

◁ *Out of the race, Vasquez struggles to hold Ruffian while Foolish Pleasure gallops for the finish line.*
N.Y. Daily News Photo

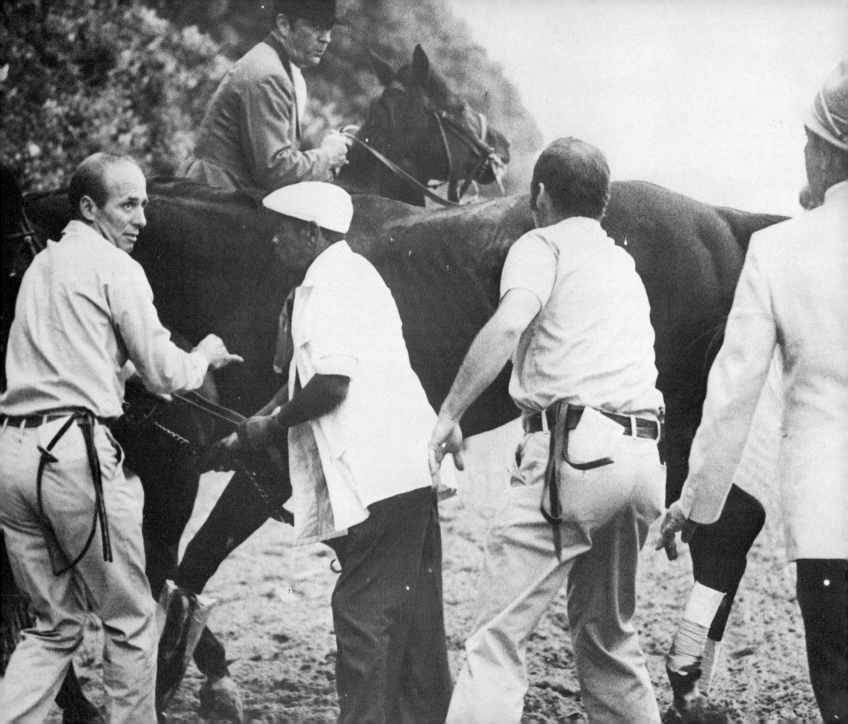

Can They Save Her?

In her own mind, Ruffian had not stopped racing. Track men, guards and assistants rushed out to help. There was little they could do, however. Even Dan Williams could not calm her. She wanted to finish the race. In every fiber of her body, she wanted to pass that other horse, take the lead, and win. Now she was hobbled to the earth. The men around her wanted Ruffian to stand still. For her it was like being strangled alive.

While the men tried to calm the filly, Dr. Gilman prepared a pneumatic cast. It was a kind of thick balloon, shaped like a hollow tube, with a zipper up the side. Dr. Gilman put the plastic around the filly's leg and zipped up the side. Then he pumped air into it until the bone was held rigid.

When the cast was on, the men helped Ruffian as she tried to stand on four legs again. She was a little calmer. But it wasn't her usual, proud calmness. It was more as if she were dazed. She didn't seem to recognize Dan.

Dr. Gilman knew Ruffian was in a state of severe shock. Her whole body was reacting to the terrible wound in her leg, rushing to keep up with the loss of blood. The injury was already taking too much out of her. To bring her back, the doctor knew, they would have to do something soon.

Calming her with word and touch, Dan and the other men helped Ruffian onto the ambulance. Dan worked with the horse as he always had, one step at a time. There was a difference though. He had to impose his will on her, for her own sake.

Perhaps it was this she resisted most of all. She was still stronger than any man.

◁ *Dan Williams urges Ruffian to turn, while track workers assist.*   United Press International Photo

That strength threatened to go wild. Dan had to be strict with her and she had to obey. That was most urgent.

The ambulance drove to Stable 34.

Ruffian was still bleeding. It was building up inside the balloon-like cast. Suddenly, the inside of the cast burst from the pressure of the blood.

Hurriedly, Dr. Gilman put on a second cast. Ruffian was still standing.

At the stable, Mr. Whiteley directed the men as they helped Ruffian from the ambulance. She could not walk by herself. Urging her, half-carrying her, the men took her out of the ambulance.

That stable became the scene of a long, bitter struggle. Ruffian was going through cycles of shock and pain. They had to cool her off somehow.

Dr. Prendergast and Dr. Harthill joined Dr. Gilman at the stable. The doctors treated her with several needle-shots of drugs that would cool her off and ease the pain. They decided to take Ruffian into her stable. Frank Whiteley and Dan Williams joined hands under her belly. Dr. Harthill and Yates Kennedy lifted her rump. Together the four men half-carried Ruffian into her stall.

In the stall, Dr. Prendergast took x-rays, then raced to the clinic to have them developed.

The wait seemed endless. Mr. Whiteley directed some of the hands to bring ice water. They filled tub after tub with water, bathing Ruffian's leg while they held her up. The drugs and ice treatment were taking effect and she was cooling off. Now she wanted to lie down.

The men struggled to keep her standing. Once she was down, she might never get up again. They couldn't risk it.

Dr. Prendergast returned with the x-rays, still wet from the developing room. The pictures told them the worst. Both sesamoids were broken.

Frank Whiteley looked grim. He had hoped the x-rays would show them some reason to hope. Now, he knew, there was little chance of saving her.

◁ *Dr. Gilman with Ruffian. He put on a pneumatic cast filled with air that helped her stand on the injured leg.* United Press International Photo

Dan led Ruffian up the ramp into the ambulance. Track workers stood clear as the filly staggered.   N.Y. Daily News

   Mr. Whiteley met with Mr. Janney and the doctors. Ruffian's chances, according to the doctors, were less than one in ten. She continued in shock and she'd lost a great deal of blood. No one knew what would happen if they tried surgery. Nevertheless it was clear she needed the operation if she was going to live. The leg would never heal by itself.

   Even if the operation were successful, she would never run again. Running wasn't important anymore. Ruffian was a horse with a great spirit. If there was any earthly way to save her, then they wanted her to live.

   Every moment brought more pain and misery to her. It might be an unjust cruelty to keep her alive. Surgery might be successful. Yet if the operation failed, she would suffer needlessly.

   ◁ *Wracked with pain, the filly lunges forward.*   United Press International Photo

It was a terribly difficult decision those men had to make. The horse had given everything for them. In return, they had cared for her as well as men care for any beautiful horse. Now she needed their skill, the power of their judgment. Beside her they felt a little helpless, as if this was something she should not have asked of them. They needed courage that could match hers.

They decided to operate.

"Go as far as you can and do the best you can," Mr. Janney said to Dr. Harthill.

Mr. Whiteley turned away from the meeting of men and he looked at the horse. Her eyes were glazed with pain and she seemed ready to collapse.

Usually Mr. Whiteley didn't second-guess when he'd made a decision. But he felt a twinge of doubt. Had they done the right thing?

Something deep inside him, some sense that came from years of living with horses, told him that she wouldn't make it. But that was only instinct. He couldn't explain it very well. He certainly wouldn't feel right asking for her death.

The doctors said there was a chance. Mr. Janney had given the go-ahead. So be it. Could they save her?

Mr. Whiteley came toward Ruffian and the horse raised her head to him.

Yes, it might be possible. One chance in ten was enough.

The trainer looked over at Dan Williams.

Dan was busy every moment. He poured ice in the bucket. He brushed the straw out of the way with his hands. He talked to the filly and pushed against her sweaty, heaving flanks when it looked like she might go down. He kept so busy he didn't have to say anything to anyone or look anyone in the eye.

But with all that activity, he couldn't cover up the way he was feeling. The sadness was written all over his face.

The hours that followed were a nightmare that seemed to go on and on.

Once again there was the ordeal of getting Ruffian into the ambulance. She had to be taken to the nearest place where they could perform surgery. That was Dr. William Reed's Equine Hospital, right outside the stable area.

Frank Whiteley, Dan Williams, and the doctors gathered around Ruffian in the

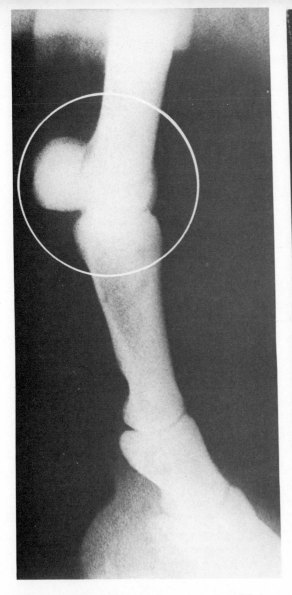 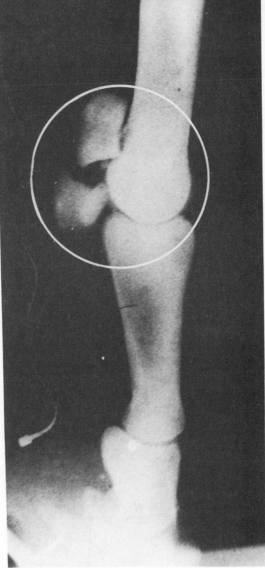

X-rays of the right front leg of a normal horse, showing the bones around the lower joints. The sesamoids (at left, inside the circle) are a pair of knob-like bones just behind the fetlock joint. In this side view, only one of the sesamoids can be seen.

X-rays of Ruffian's right front leg after she broke down. In the picture, the broken sesamoid appears as two jagged pieces of bone. Without the support of this small bone, the joint was useless and the leg collapsed.

United Press International Photo

operating room. They did their best to console the suffering filly but the shock and pain were becoming more intense with every passing moment.

Preparations began. They gave her large doses of drugs, anesthetics that would help her sleep through the operation. As she calmed down, they strapped her onto the huge surgical table.

There was a moment of panic. Her breathing and heartbeat had stopped. For an instant she hovered on the point of death.

Quickly, the doctors gave her artificial respiration to get her breathing again. They placed a mask over her muzzle. A rush of oxygen filled her lungs. They plunged a needle into her and the drugs sped through her blood. She came back, breathing again.

But her body needed a steady flow of blood and oxygen. Her whole system was going up and down like a seesaw. Before they operated, that seesaw would have to level out.

Finally, it did. She began breathing more easily. Her heartbeat was regular. She lay on her side in a deep sleep, resting at last from the unfinished race.

In some ways, an operation is a very mechanical thing. The patient is asleep in a steady state, with the body working fairly normally. The surgeon has tools to work with and he knows what must be fixed. With steady hands and skillful work, he performs the repair job well. Like a good machine, the patient's body begins working again.

With Ruffian, the doctors also had to solve the engineering problem. She would have to stand up again soon after the operation was finished. The doctors needed more than a cast. They wanted a brace that would hold the weight of her body when she stood up again. Dr. Keefer was asked to help.

Edward Keefer was a medical doctor from New York Hospital. He had built casts for many kinds of human injuries. While the operation continued, he started work on the cast that would support Ruffian.

First he designed a special shoe with bolts in it. He used a metal bar up the back of the leg and attached it with the bolts. When the surgery was over, the supporting bar would be sealed with plaster and allowed to dry solid.

The surgeons began their work. They cut into Ruffian's foreleg and removed the bits of shattered bone. They put drains under the skin to carry away the fluids. They probed for the tiny fragments of bone that were lodged in the joint and tendons.

Dan Williams and Frank Whiteley were not looking solely at a repair job. They watched the horse. They knew the final choice was up to her.

When Ruffian came out of her sleep, she would be herself again. Though she wouldn't be the horse that had run, her spirit would return to her. The will to survive, like the will to run, would come back, and there would be the light of intelligence in her eyes.

On her leg she would feel the strange weight of the cast. She would see the bright lights and the people around her. Some of it she might understand—a touch, or the sound of a familiar voice. Yet without the understanding of words, there was no way she could comprehend all of it. She might decide to fight.

If she kicked the cast away, it would be the end.

When the operation was over and the cast in place, the doctors wheeled Ruffian to the recovery room. She had been asleep on her side for more than two hours. Soon after she came out of it, she would have to stand up.

Mr. Janney thanked the doctors for their efforts and went home to await the news. Dr. Harthill went to Esposito's Tavern to wait out the early hours of the morning.

But Frank Whiteley and Dan Williams stayed close by Ruffian.

In the parking lot outside the hospital, stablehands, trainers and track people stood around talking quietly. A waiter from the Belmont Diner, a friend of Frank Whiteley's, came over with forty cups of coffee. He passed the coffee around to the people who had gathered there. In a gruff voice he talked about the horse and what she meant to Frank Whiteley. Then he too waited.

After midnight, a few people drifted away. Many stayed. They were from the stables. Most had worked with horses all their lives. They knew the real crisis was yet to come. No operation could be called successful until the horse was standing again.

Finally, Ruffian began to wake up. Mr. Whiteley sent for Dr. Harthill.

Even before her eyes opened, Ruffian began struggling a little. It was a normal reaction after coming out of a deep sleep and lying so long on her side. The doctors rubbed her muscles with alcohol. They had to get her circulation going again.

The struggle became more intense. It was a bad sign. As she became more aware of things, she struggled more. She wasn't just reacting—she was doing battle.

Dan Williams was by her head.

"Slow down, hey. Not so fast, girl," he said.

Then Mr. Whiteley tried to calm her. She didn't understand and she kicked out at them.

Her hoofs beat the air. Fully awake, she reared up. There were people she recognized, others she didn't. There were familiar voices mingled with strange sounds. It was the fiercest battle of her life and she could conquer only one way. She had to fling free from the huge, clumsy chunk of steel and plaster that clung to her leg.

The men were trying to get her up. Not yet. She kicked and kicked again violently.

Dr. Harthill saw the cast move.

Then she calmed a little.

Dr. Harthill came as close as he could. He saw that the cast had slipped down a quarter of an inch. There was no way to get it back in position. If he tried to push it on, she would kick his brains out.

After a short interval, Ruffian began thrashing again, and when she stopped, the cast had moved down a full inch. Another struggle, and three more inches lost. The cast was starting to fall apart from her violent kicking. It was twisted and smashed and she was bleeding terribly.

The battle was over.

Dr. Harthill gave Ruffian another large dose of anesthetic and she fell asleep. He consulted Mr. Whiteley and the other doctors. Dan Williams stood aside, looking at the sleeping horse.

The discussion was brief. They all knew the alternatives. The leg was now swollen. There was tremendous bleeding. The cast was useless. Another operation would take three or four hours and the sole result might be more suffering for the filly. The alternative was death.

Horsemen call it "putting her down."

Dr. Harthill called Mr. Janney, who gave his consent.

At 2:20 a.m. on the morning of July 7, Dr. Harthill gave Ruffian a massive dose of phenobarbital. She was already asleep and the drug worked quickly. Her breathing stopped, her heart ceased pounding and the great horse lay still.

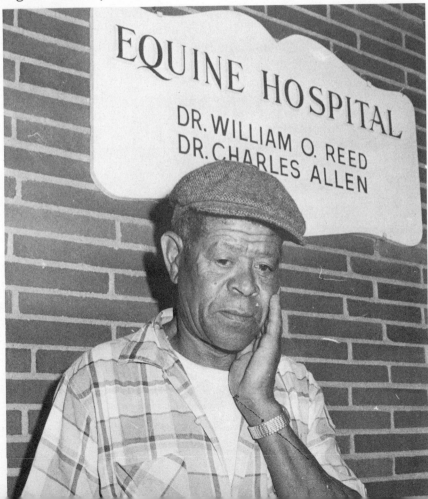

Dan Williams in front of the hospital shortly after doctors gave Ruffian the fatal dose of drugs.   Wide World Photos

A Grave and a Memory

That same morning at 4 a.m., Frank Whiteley was at Stable 34 taking care of the horses. His groom and stablehands came to work on time and they did not talk to him about Ruffian. Dan Williams filled up the water tubs and led some of the horses out for their morning exercise. The reporters were there all day asking dozens of questions.

In the afternoon, Jacinto Vasquez rode a horse in the first race and won.

Monday evening, after the races were over, a crane-shovel drove in front of the grandstand, passed the finish line and came to a stop near the flagpole. It turned onto the grass and the operator began digging a large hole, loading the soil into a dumptruck.

It was already dark when an ambulance arrived carrying the body of Ruffian. Guards formed a ring around the track area to keep out reporters and bystanders. Mr. Whiteley had asked that only the "family" of Ruffian be present.

The exercise boy and stablehands were there. Dan Williams walked from his bleak, furnished room at the stables to the racetrack. Jacinto Vasquez attended the burial with his wife. Louise Whiteley came with her husband. The Janneys arrived.

Covered with layers of canvas, the body of Ruffian was lifted from the back of the ambulance and lowered into the deep hole in the ground. Frank Whiteley was holding the blankets that had been Ruffian's. He looked around and handed them to his assistant, Mike Bell. "Here, you put them on her," he said. Mike climbed down a ladder

◁ *Only the "family" of Ruffian attended the late-night burial at Belmont Park. The horse ambulance (at left) brought her body to the infield.*
United Press International Photo

and laid the blankets over the head and shoulders of the great horse. Then he climbed out again.

Ruffian was buried with her head toward the finish line. Many wept.

Two stablehands threw red roses on top of the freshly turned earth. A wreath was placed on the ground. Then, turning away, the family left Ruffian forever.

Ruffian was buried at the foot of the flagpole, yards from the finish line, with a horseshoe wreath to mark her grave. The flag of the New York Racing Association fluttered at half-mast the next day.

N.Y.R.A.—Joseph DeMaria